MW01698444

Triple No. 8

Neila Mezynski
Cooper Renner
Kathryn Rantala

The Ravenna Triple Series

Chapbooks as they were meant to be read—
in good company.

ISBN: 978-1-7326416-5-5

Published by Ravenna Press
USA
ravennapress.com

FIRST EDITION

Neila Mezynski

Recent Pieces

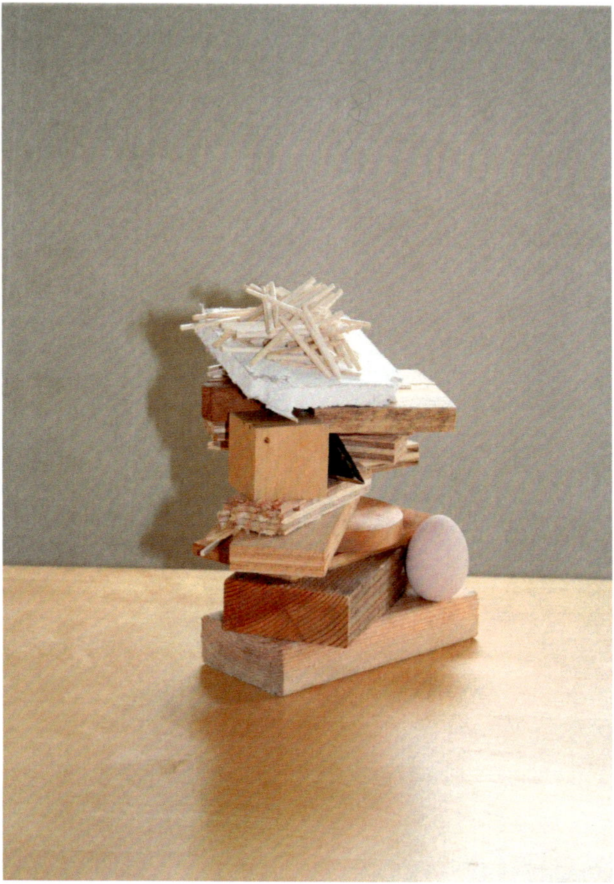

House 33

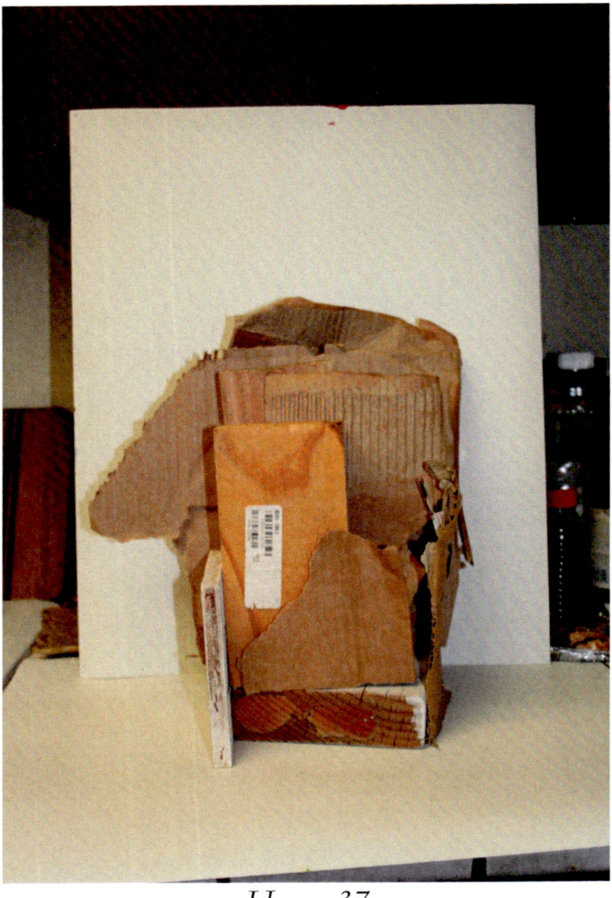

House 37

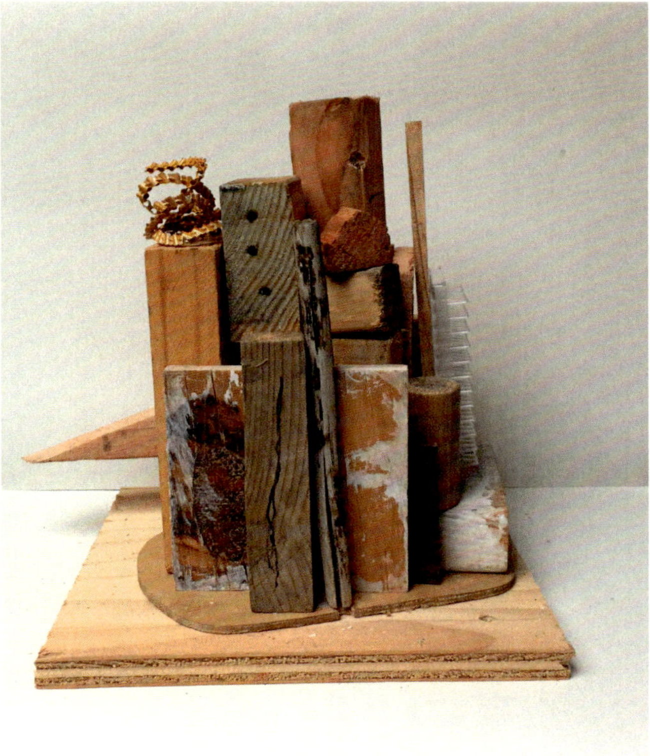

House 36

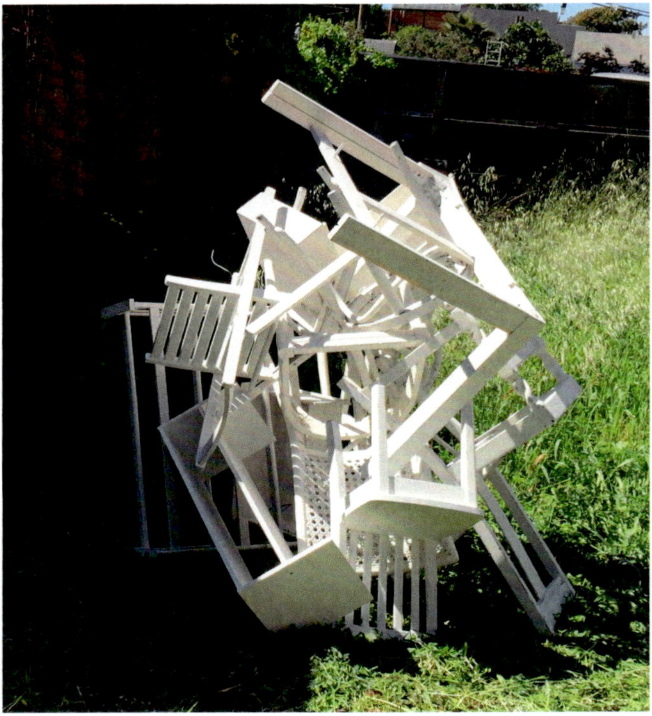

House 43

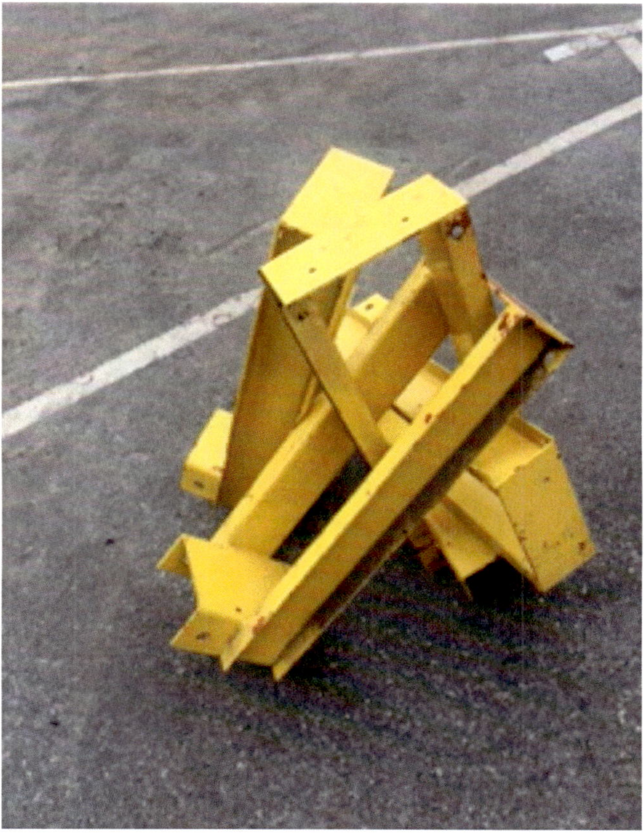

Lemon House 46

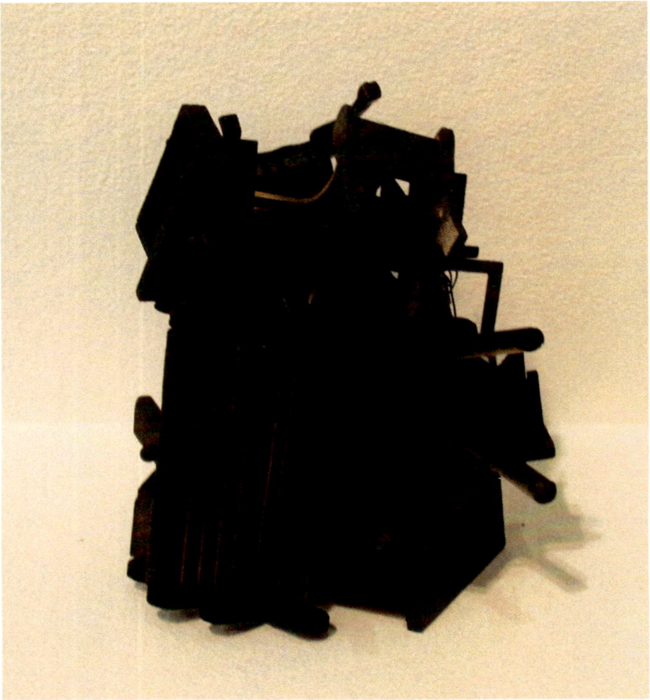

House 2

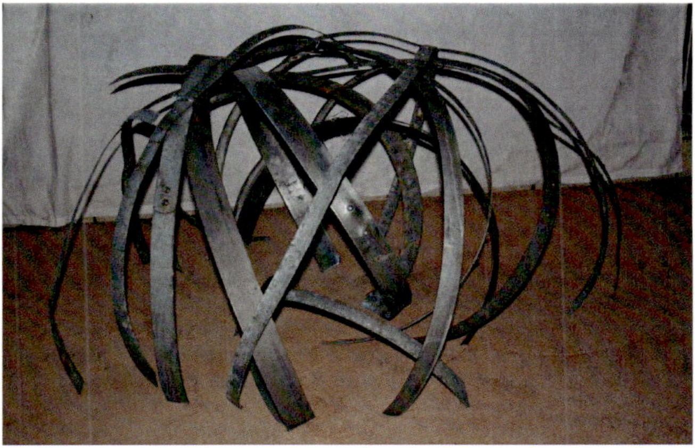

Skirt

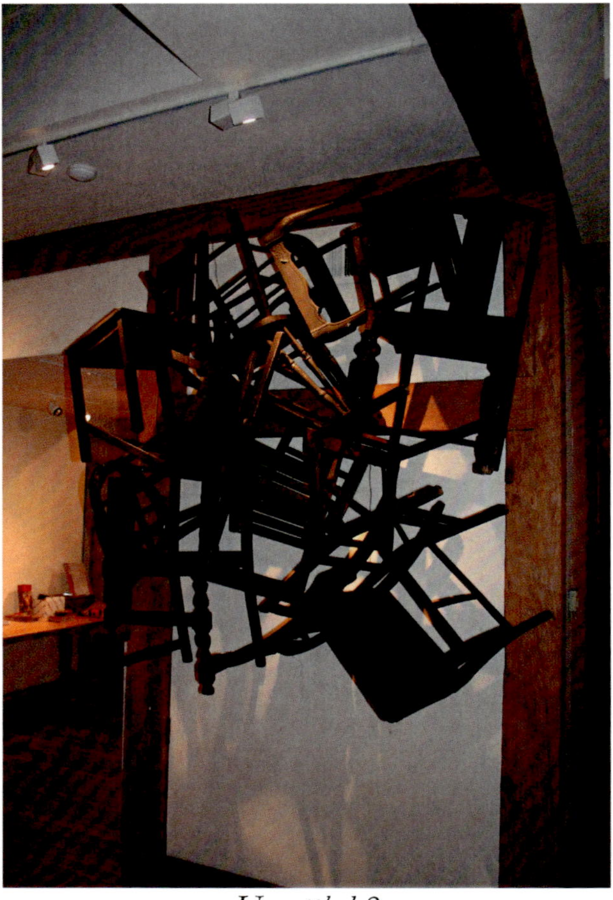

Unsettled 2

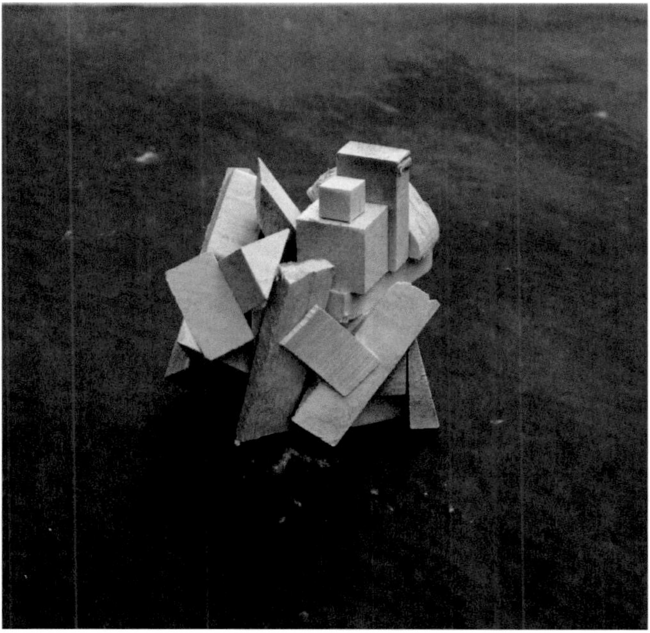

White House

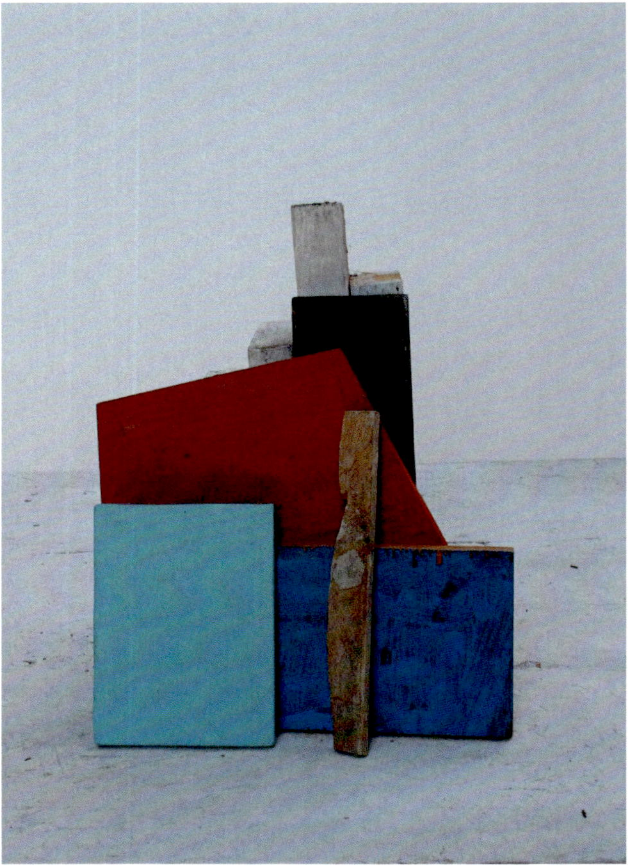

Construct

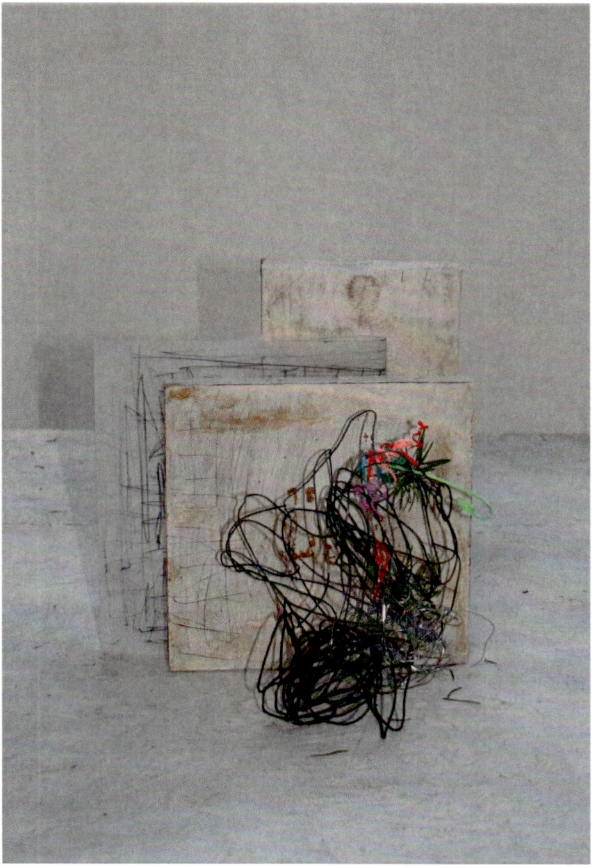

Miriam's Backyeard

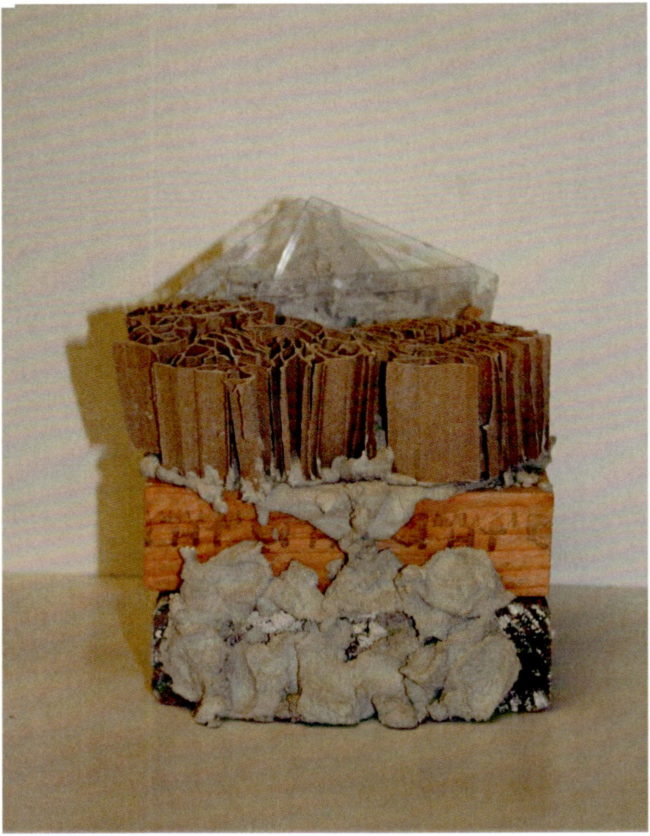

House 29

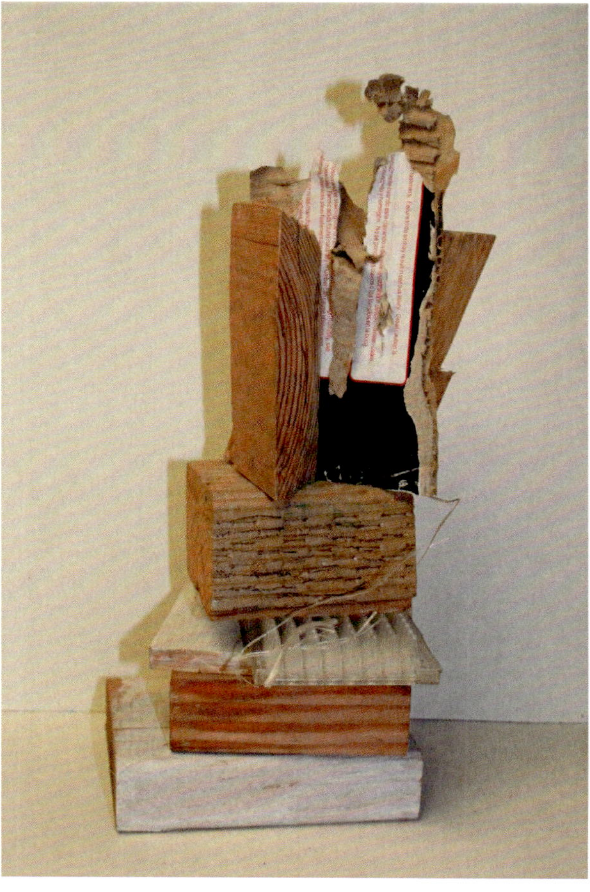

House 35

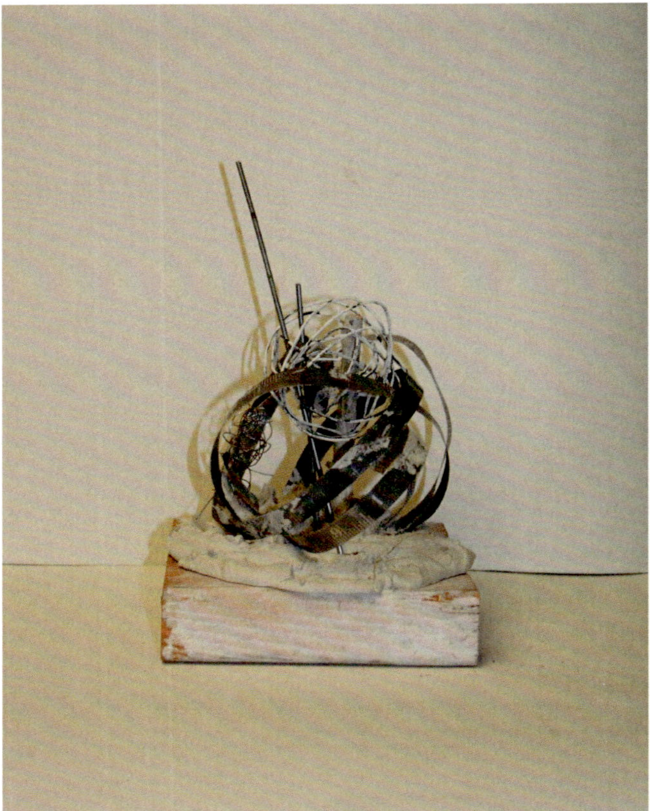

House 41

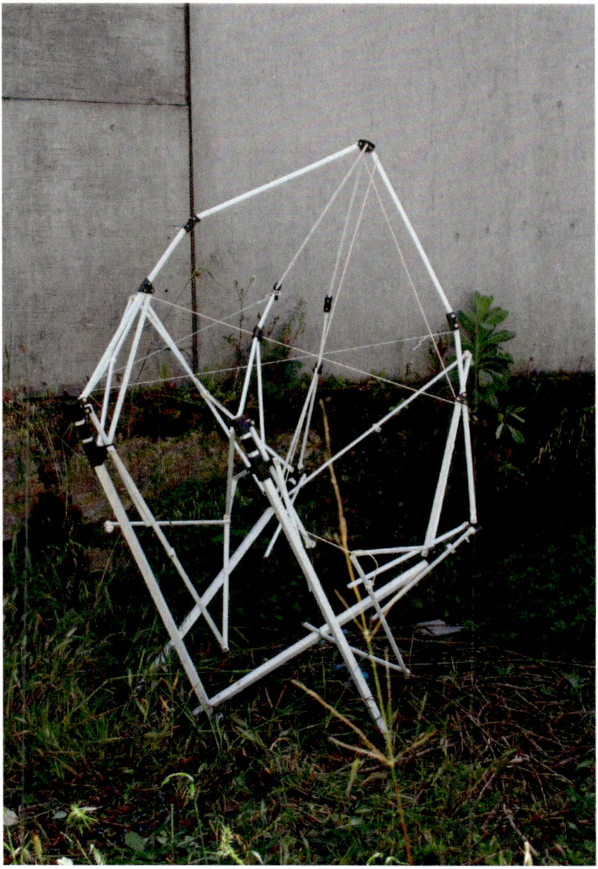

Trapezoid

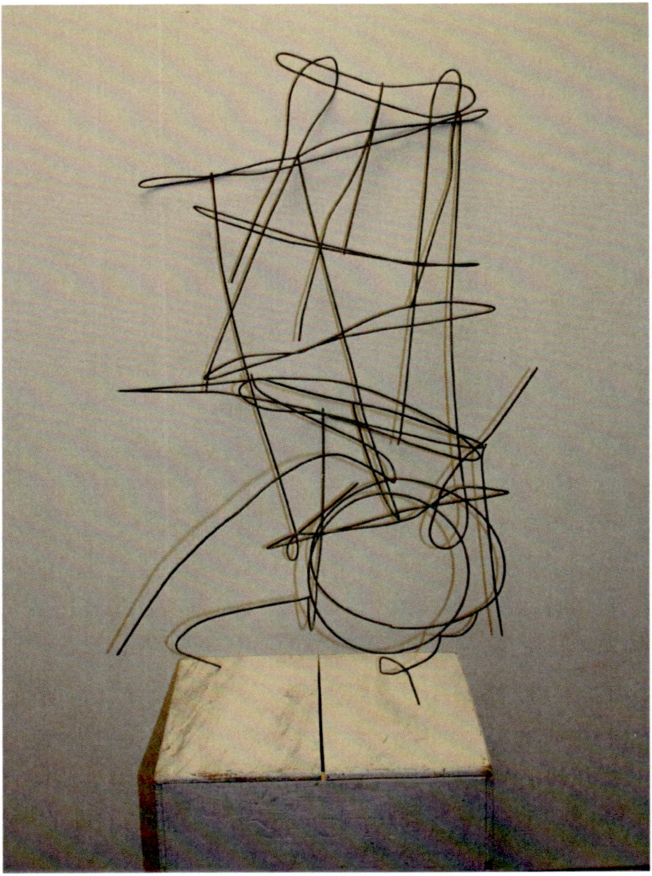

Drawing for Brian

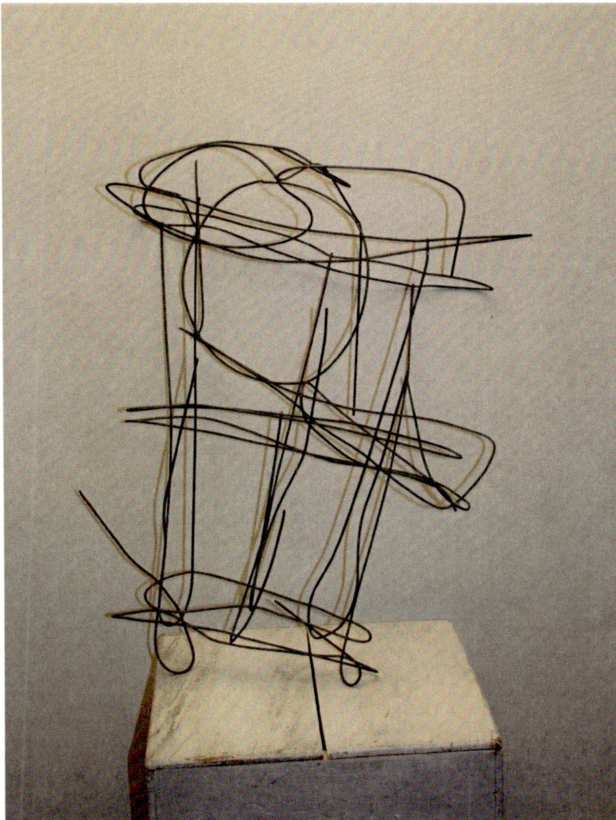

Drawing for Brian 2

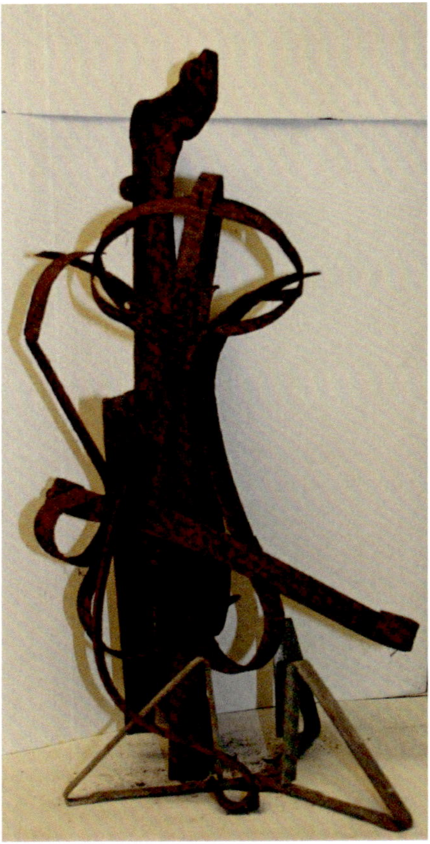

Dancer

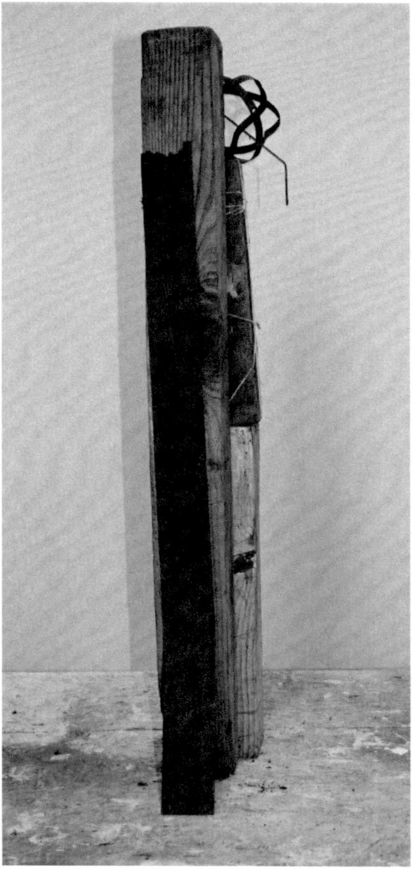

Half Hearted

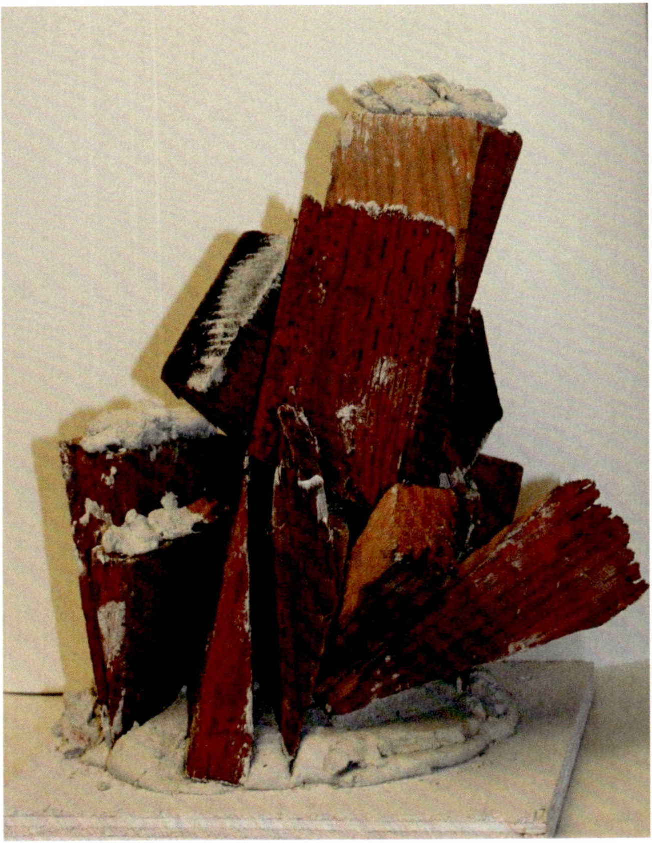

Image 5278

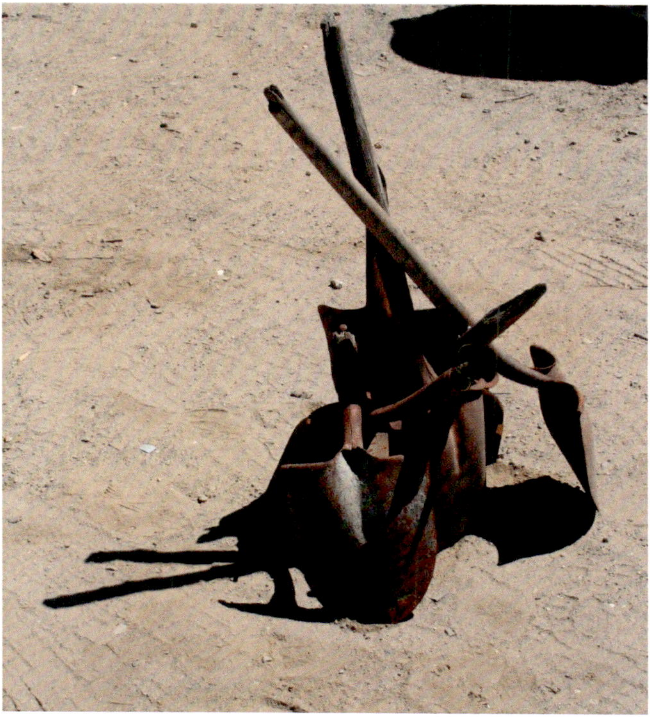

Docile

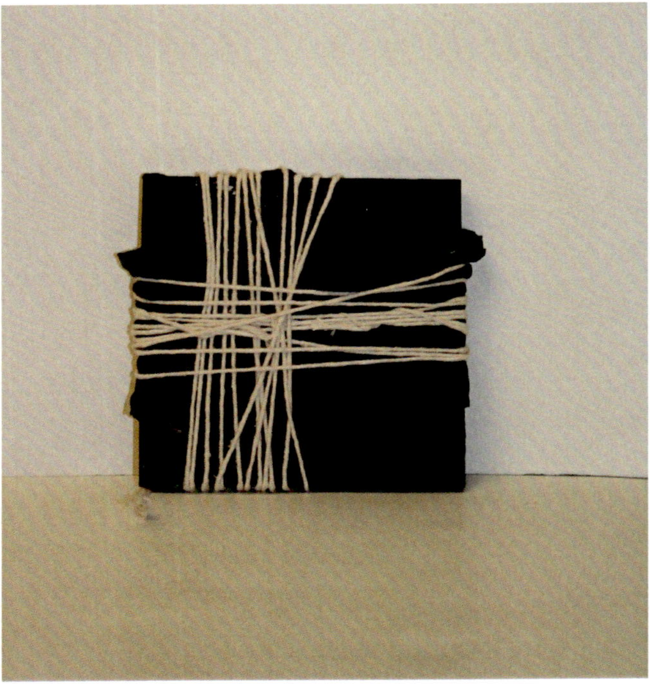

Habit

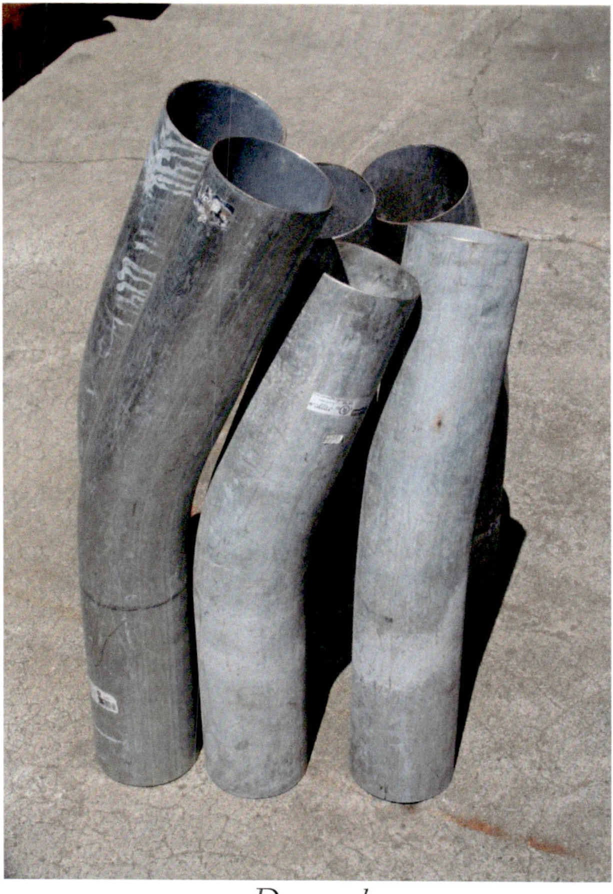

Duressed

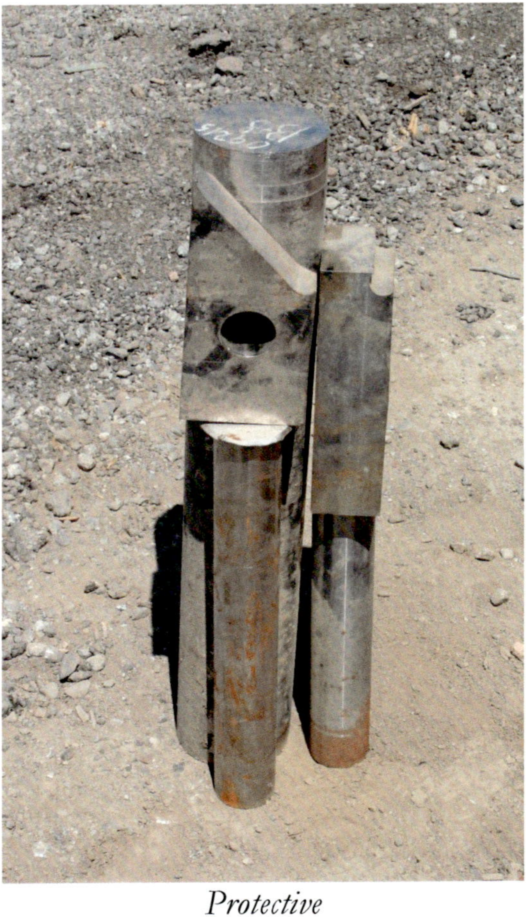

Protective

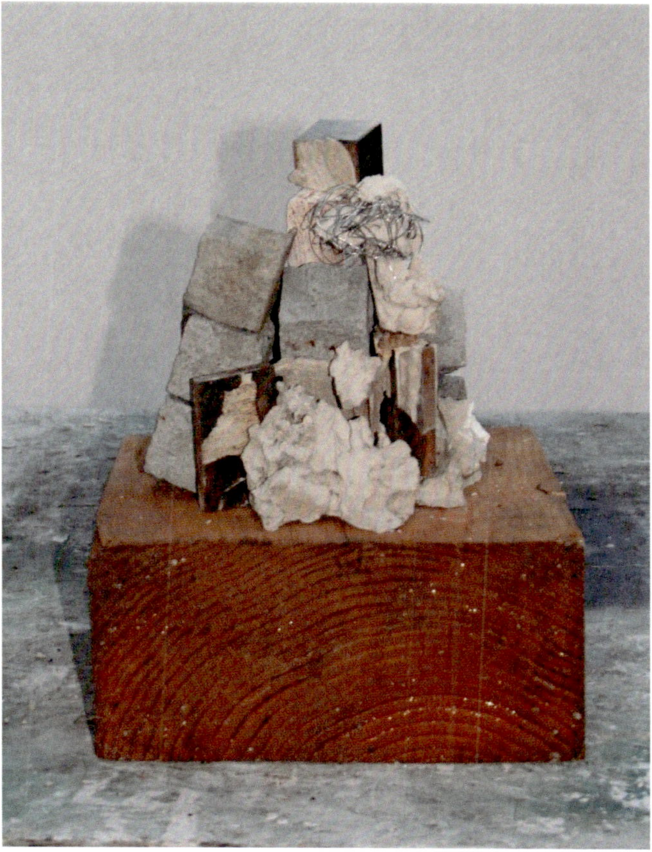

Molehill

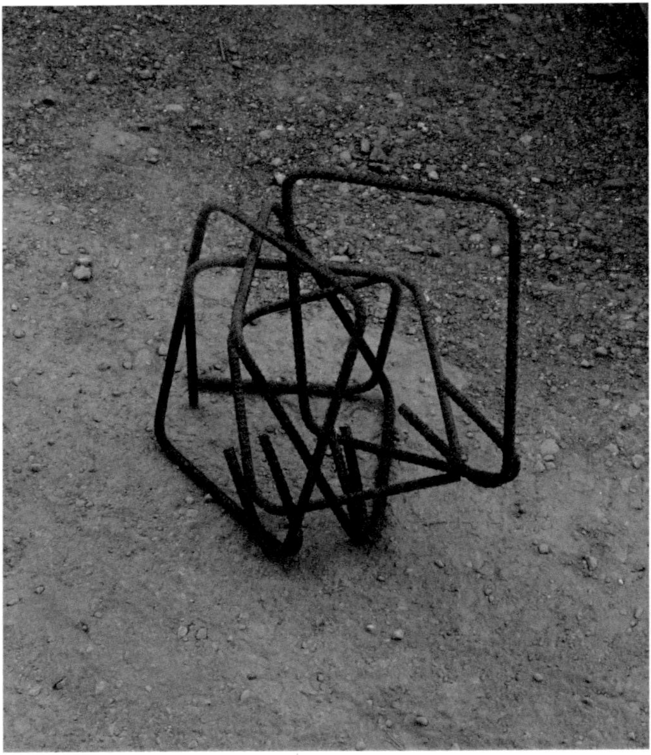

Point of View

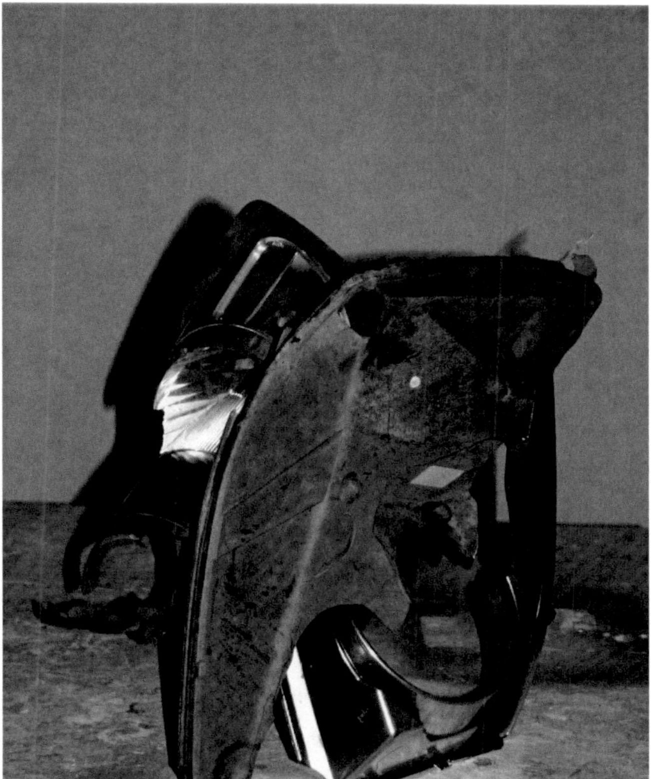

Road Kill

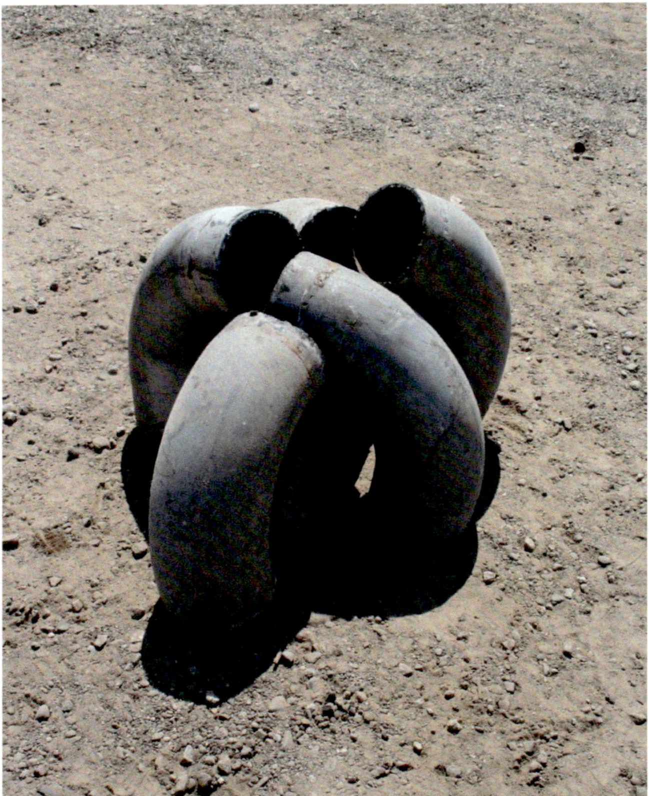

Gossips

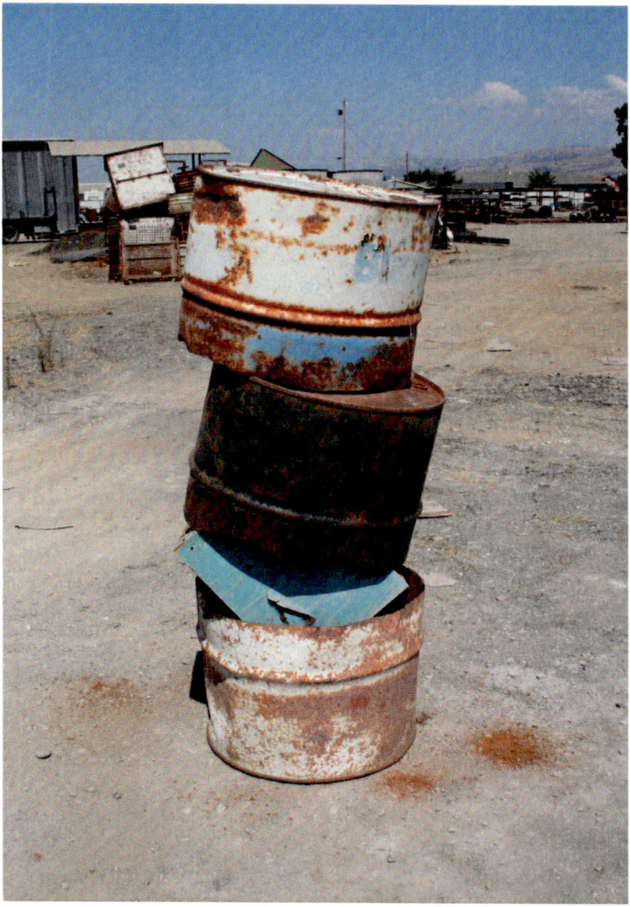

Embellished

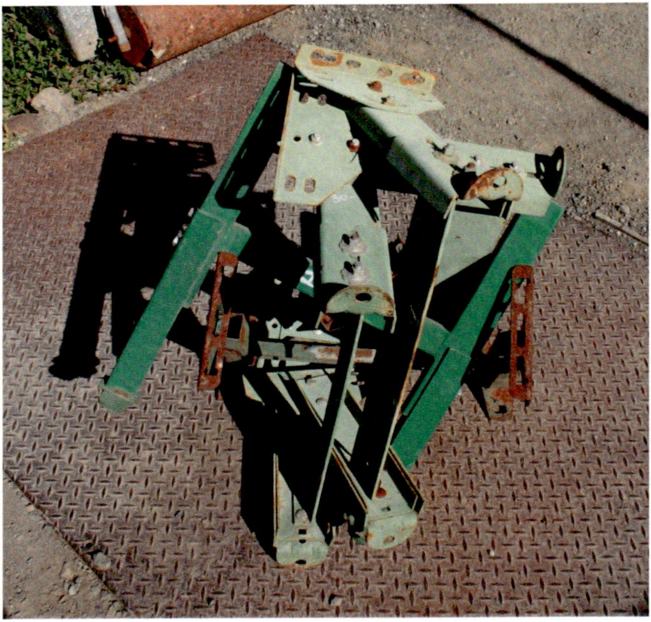

Beleaguered

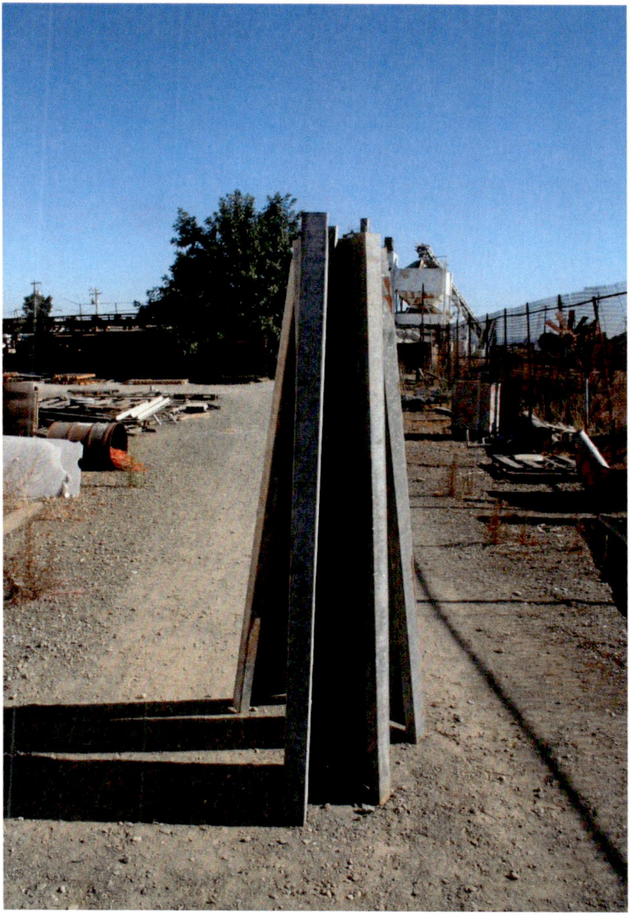

4 Tall Women

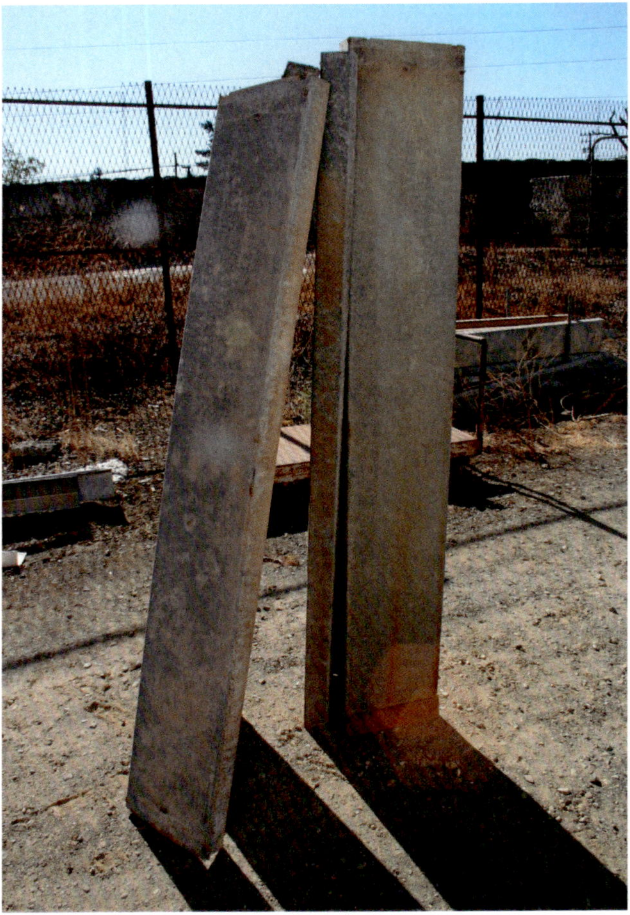

Visitor

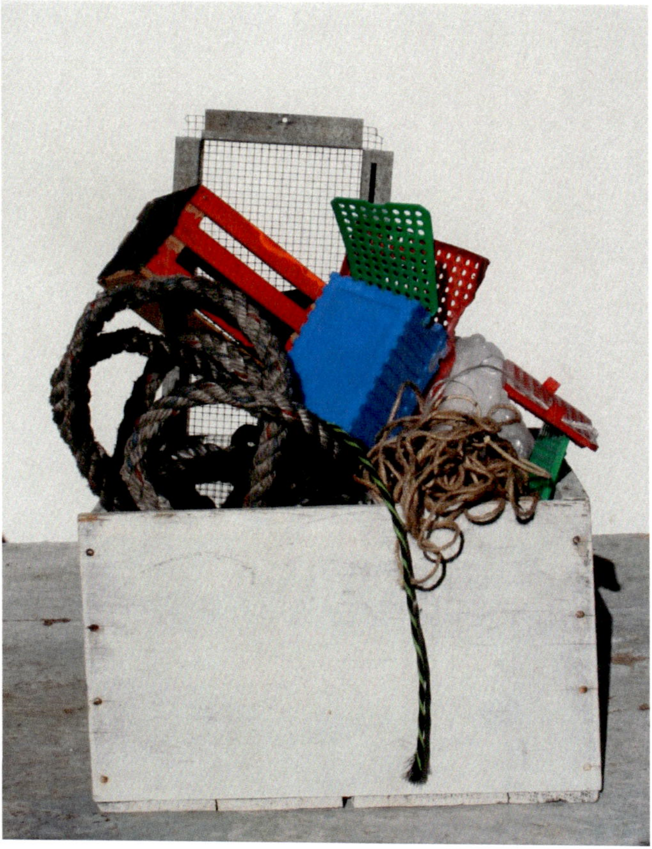

Music Box 4

Cooper Renner

I Would Prefer Not To

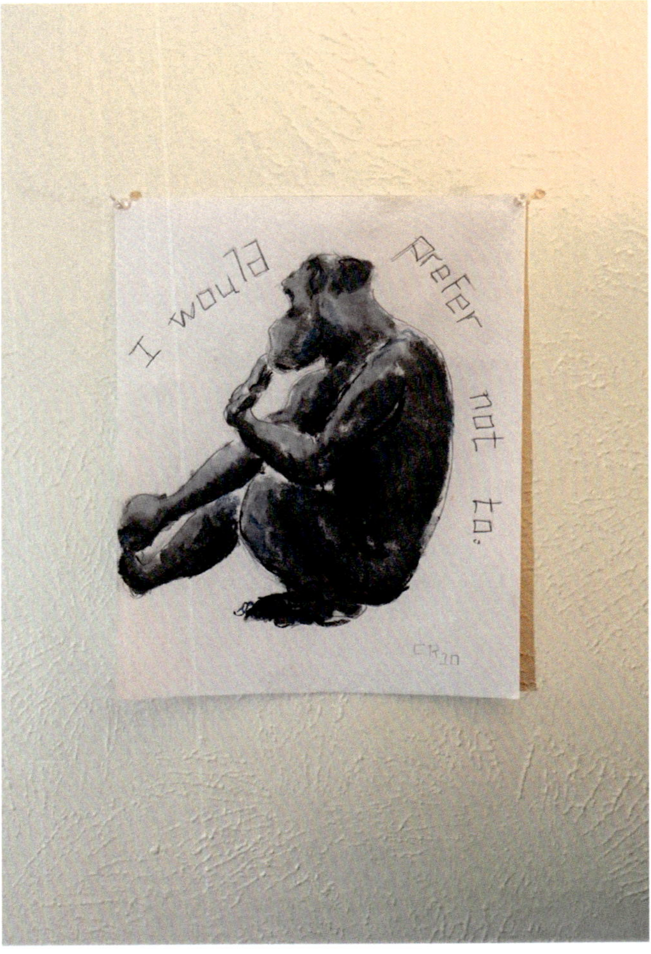
I would prefer not to.
CR10

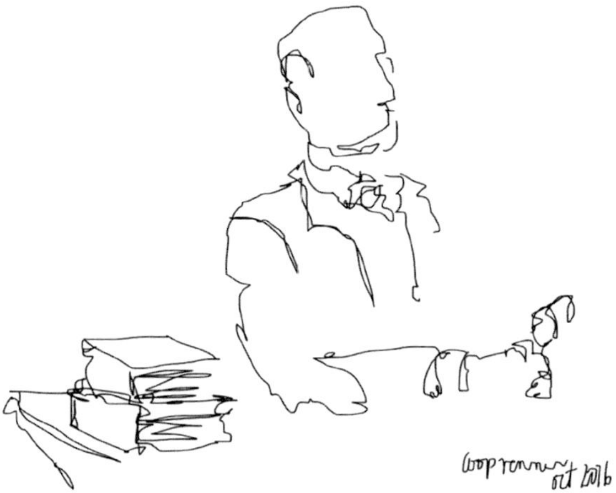

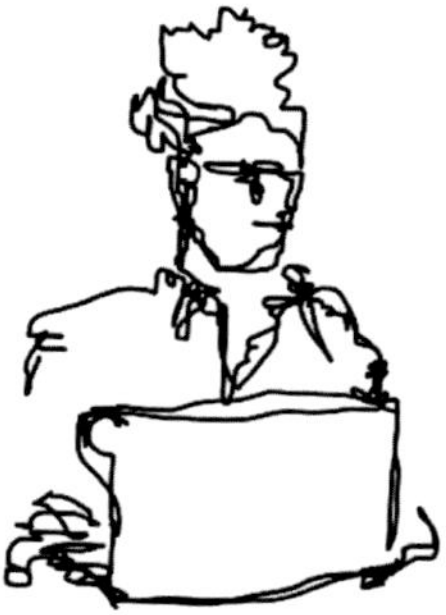

roop
renner
oct 2017

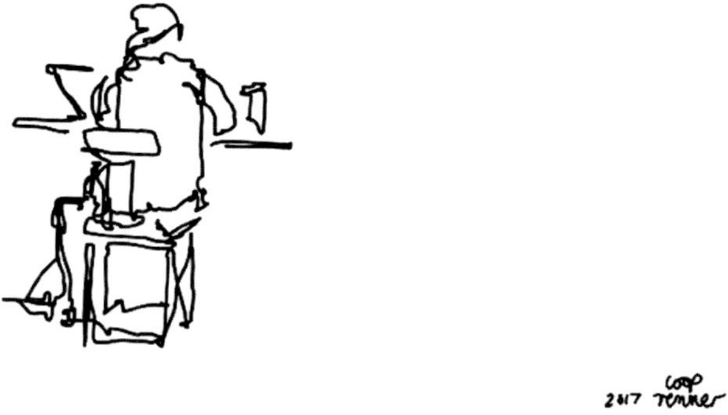
2017 coop renner

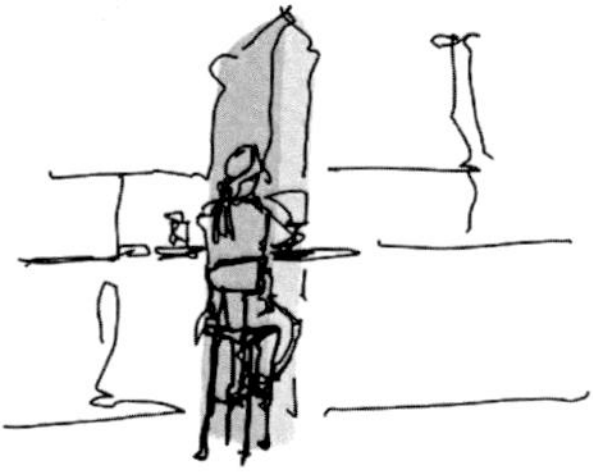

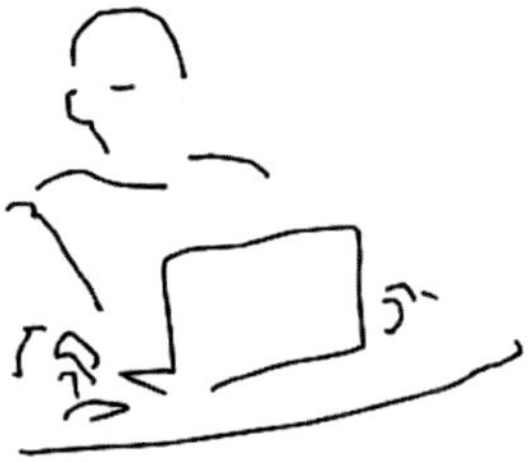

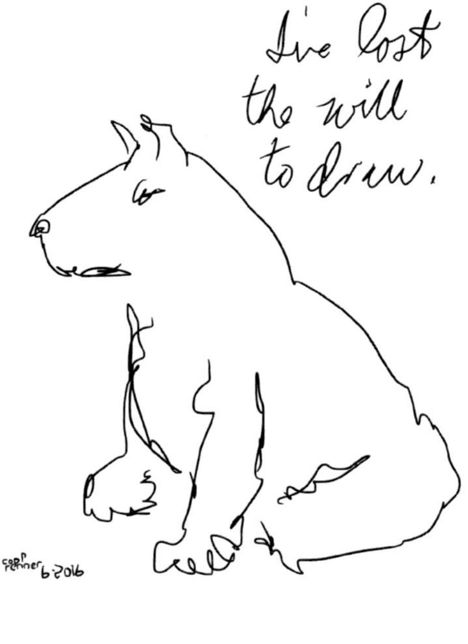
I've lost the will to draw.
renner 6-2016

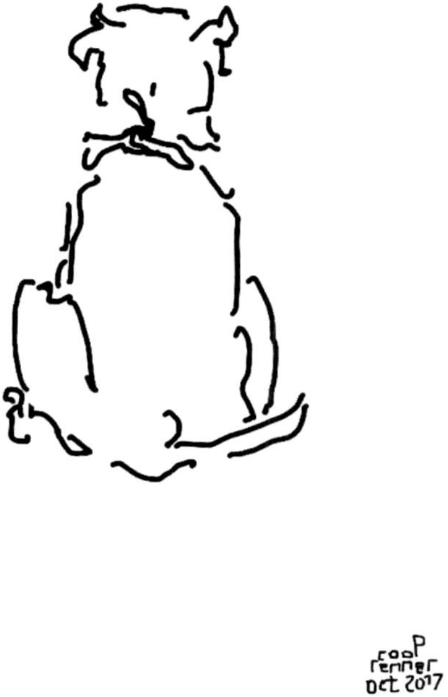
coop
renner
oct 2017

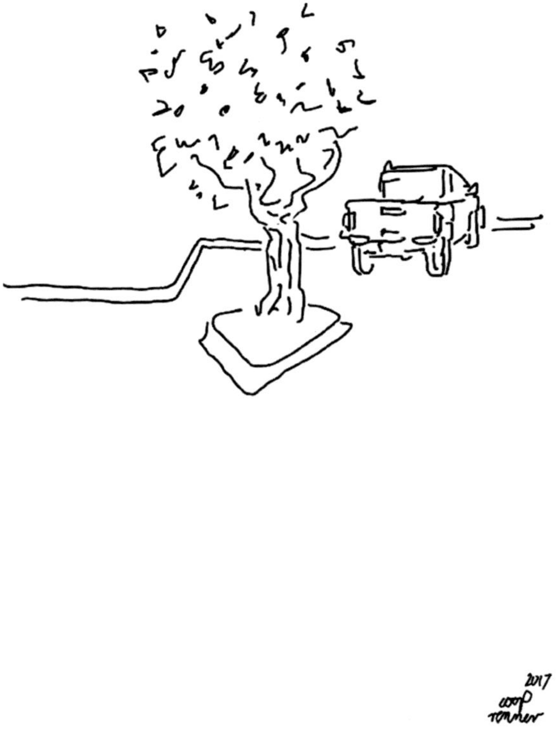
2017

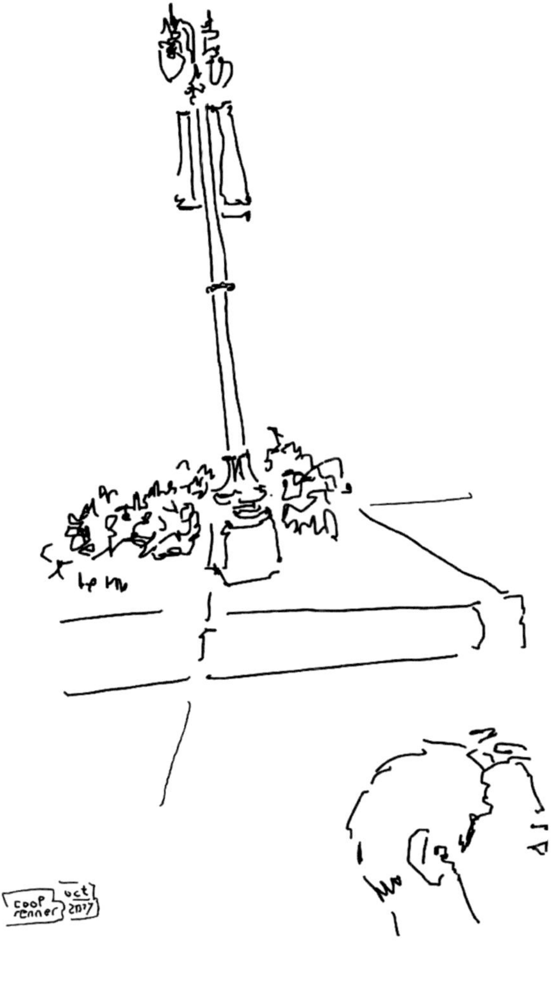
coop renner
oct 2017

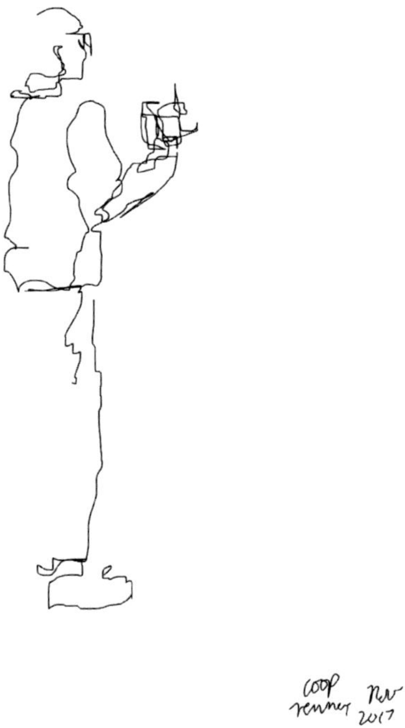
coop
renner
2017

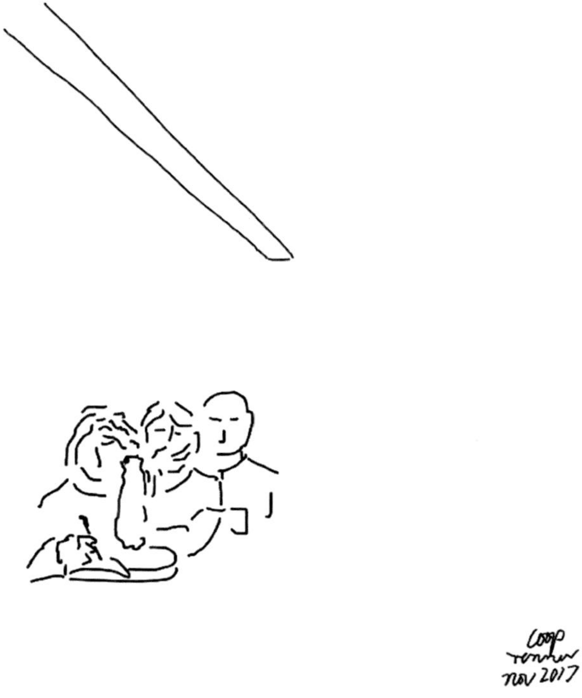

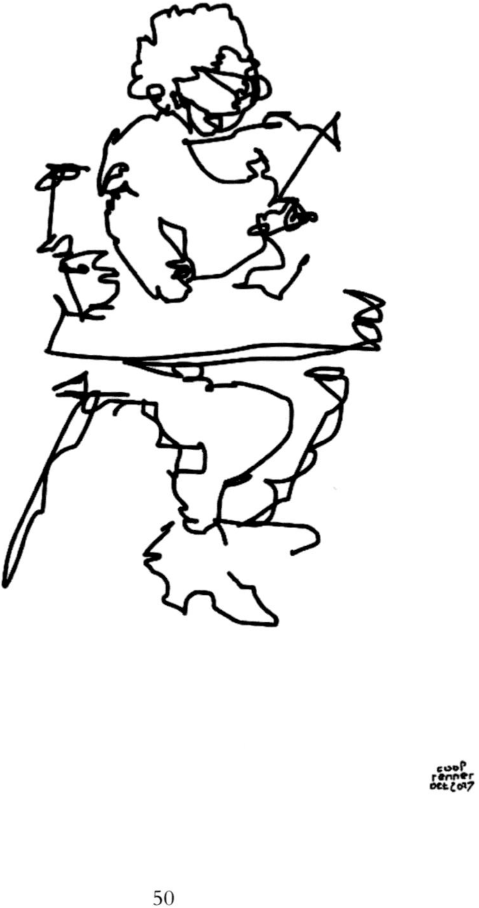
coop
renner
oct 2017

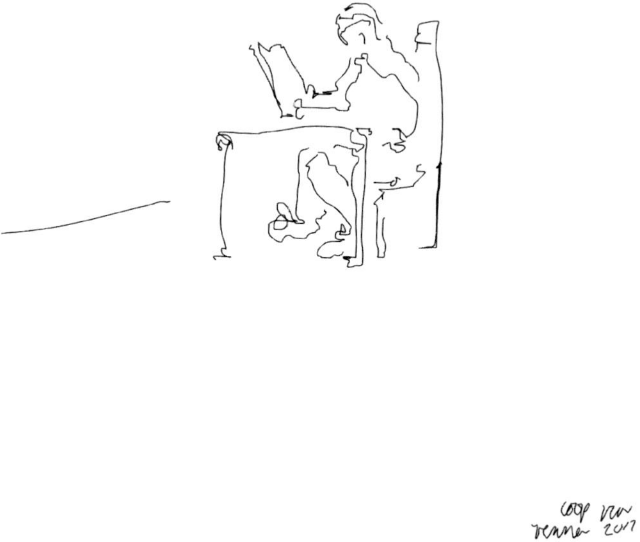

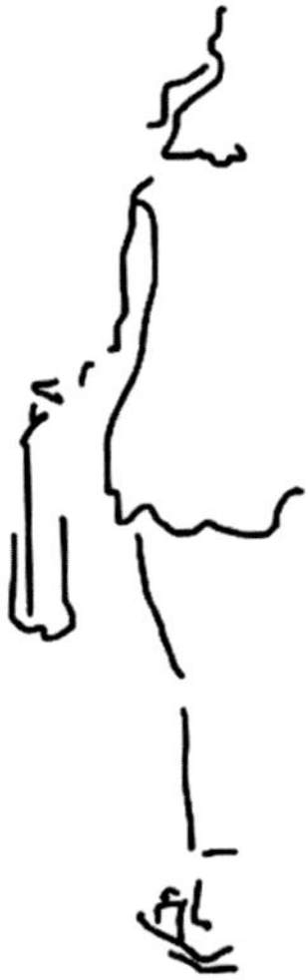

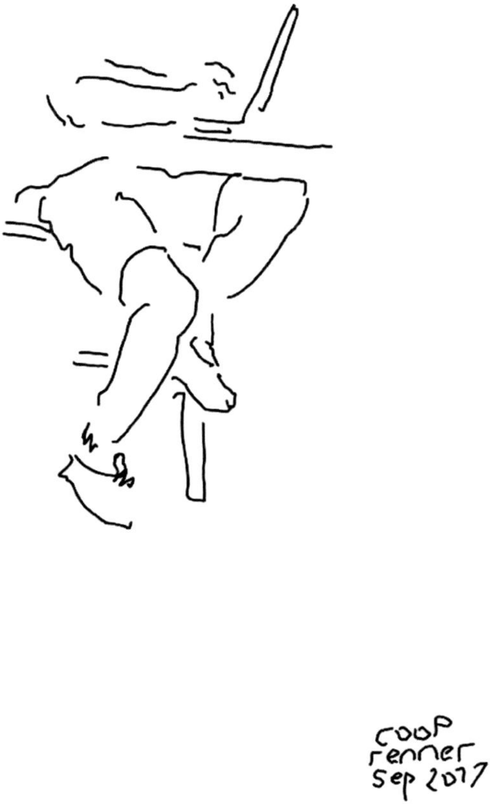
coop
renner
sep 2017

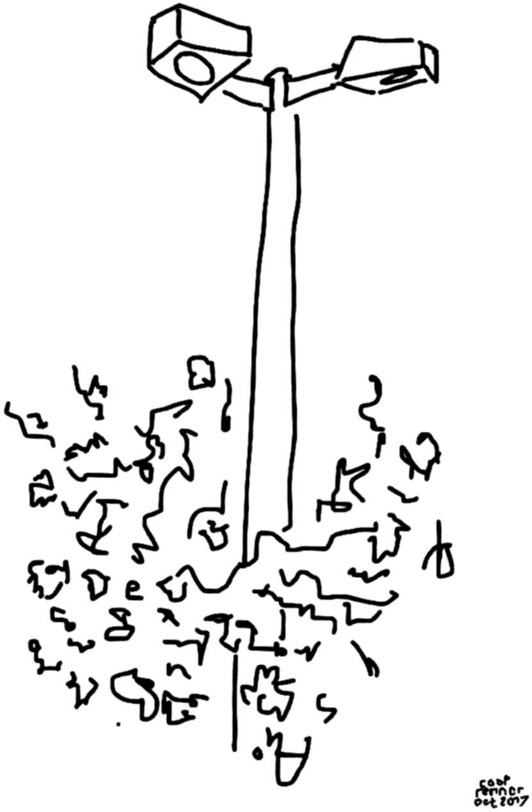
coop
renner
oct 2017

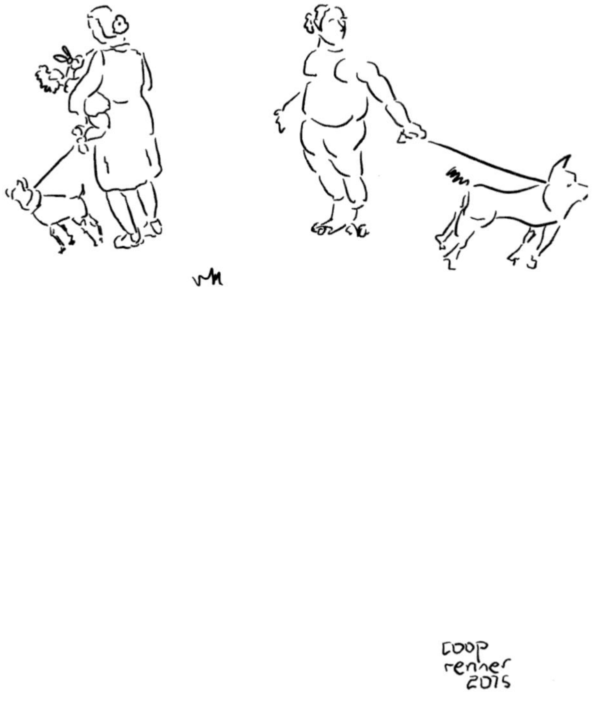
coop
renner
2015

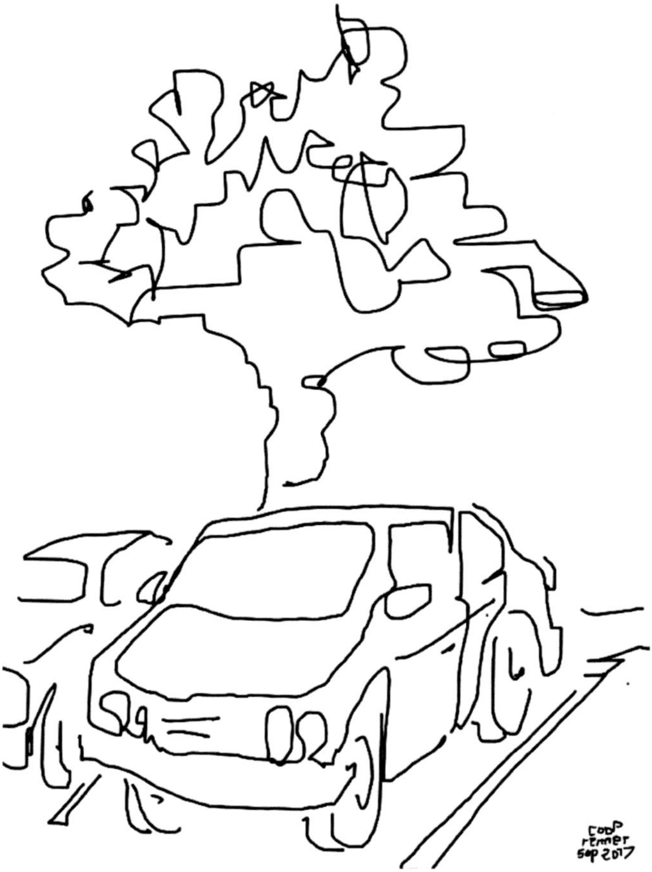
coop
renner
sep 2017

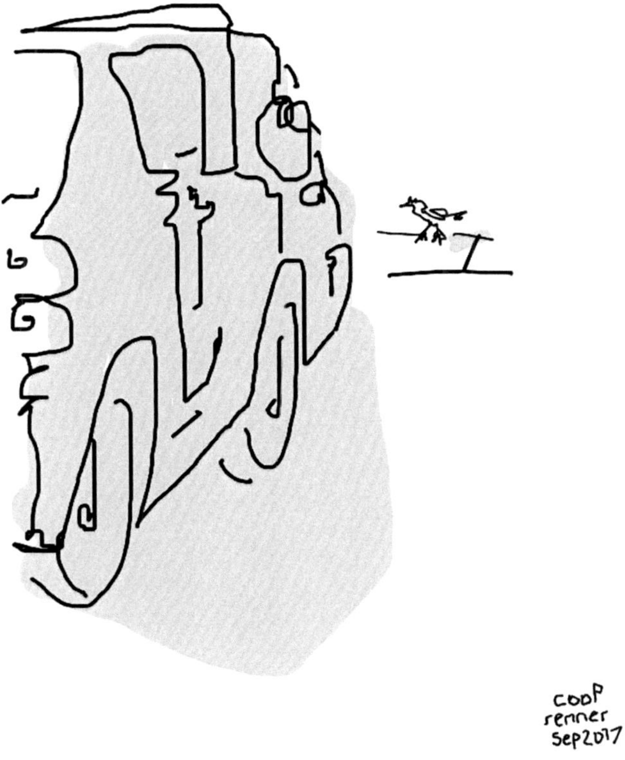
coop
renner
Sep2017

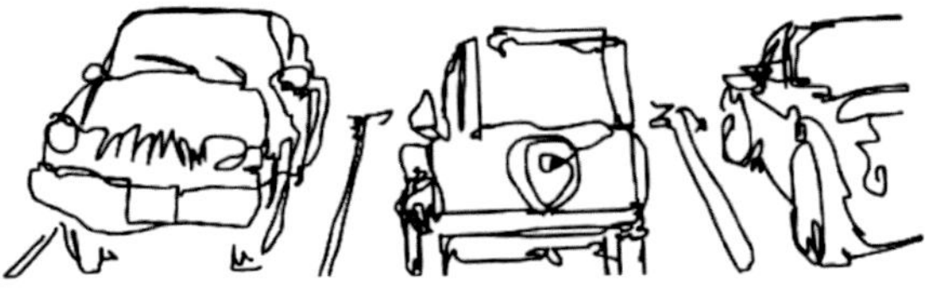

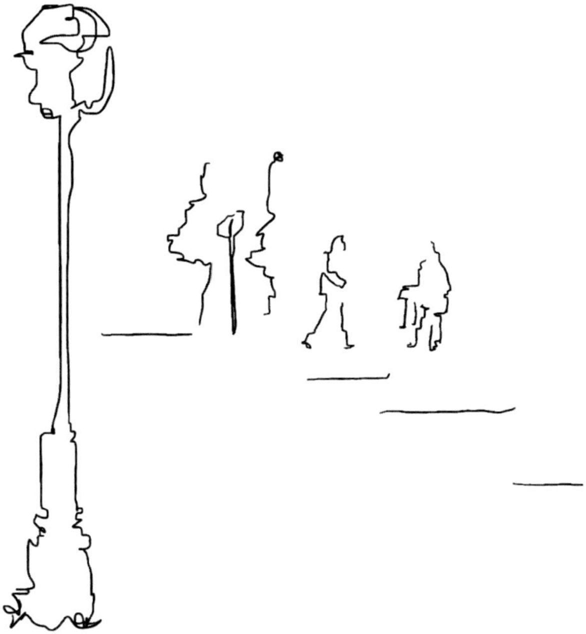

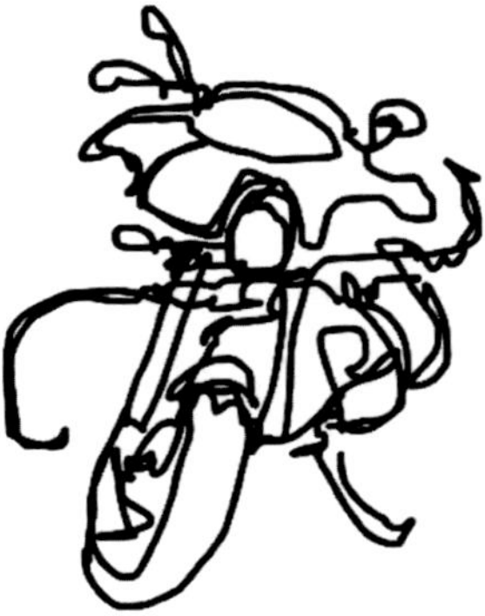

coop
renner
Sep 2017

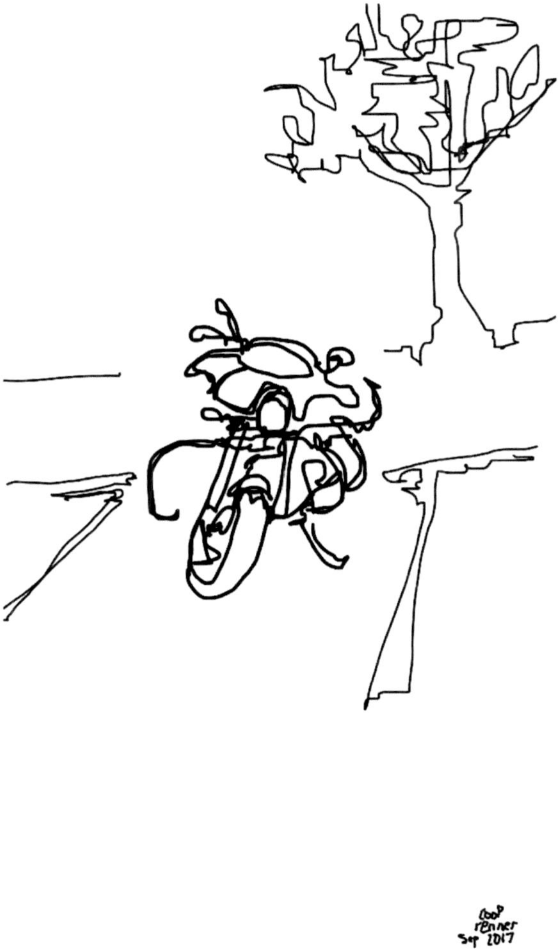
coop
renner
Sep 2017

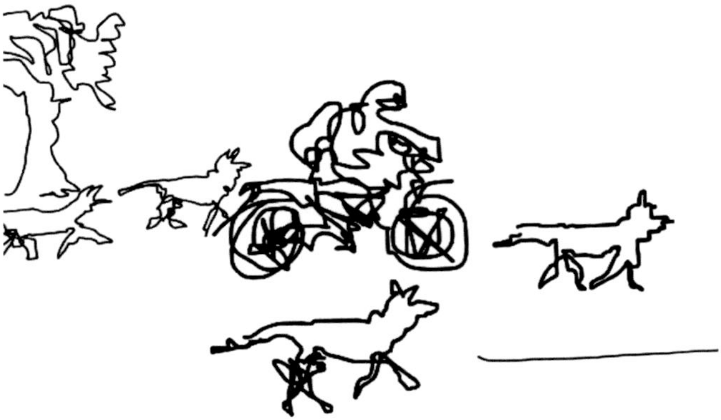

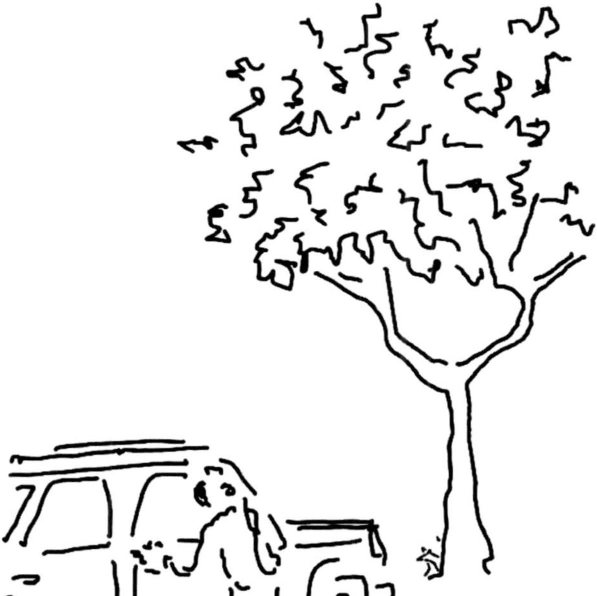
coop
renner
2017

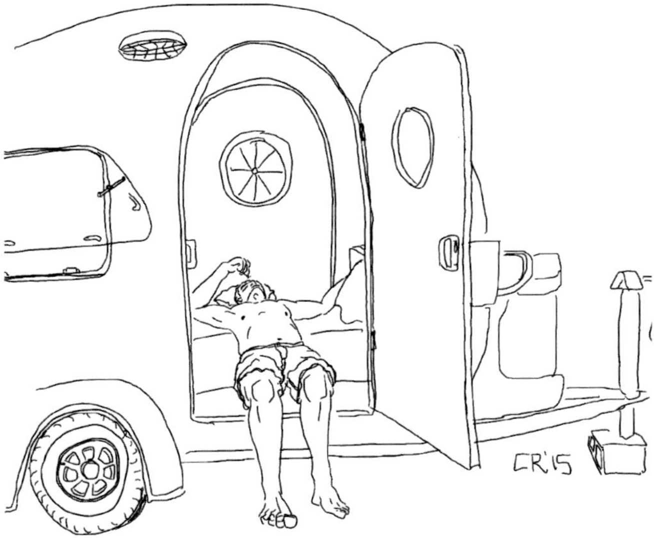
CR'15

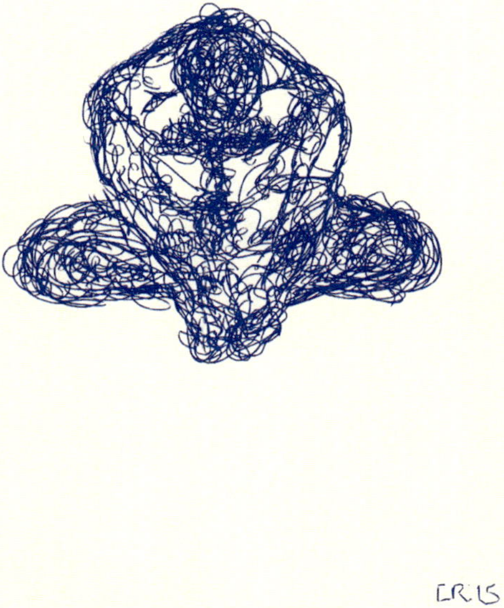
ER.15

Kathryn Rantala

Two Poems Illuminated by Assemblages

the restraint,
the hydrotensility

The Transformative Power

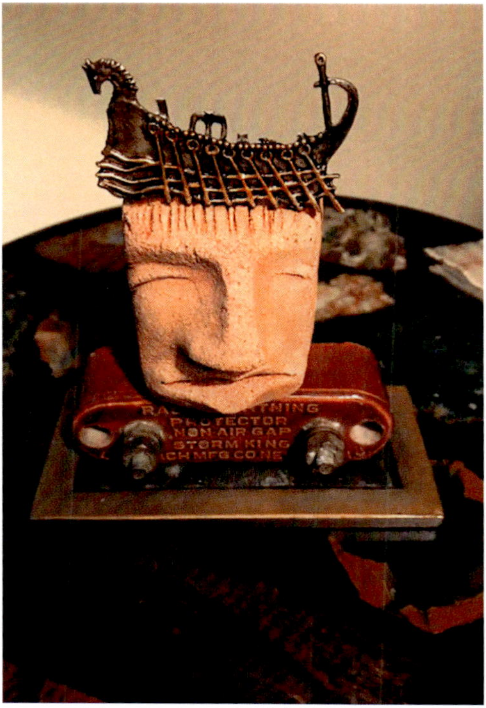

The frigate *Self*, as *Frigate*;

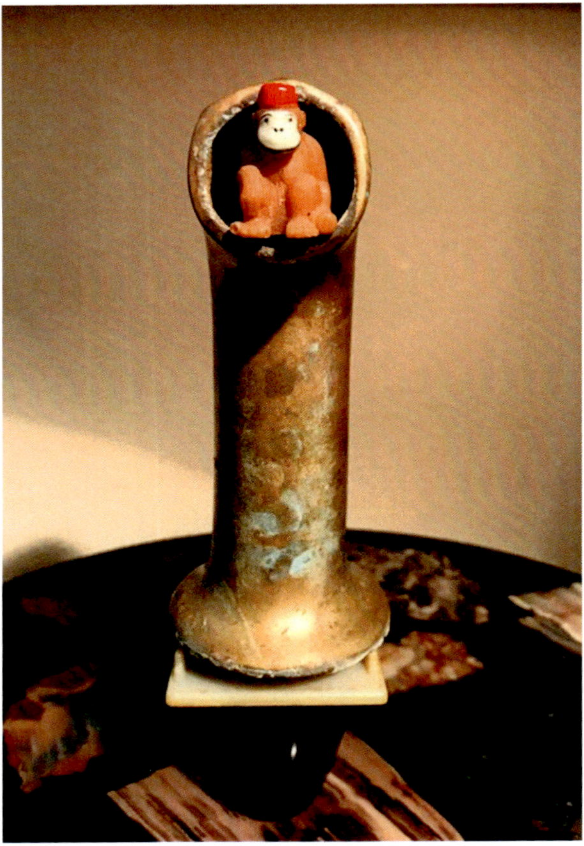

sighting,

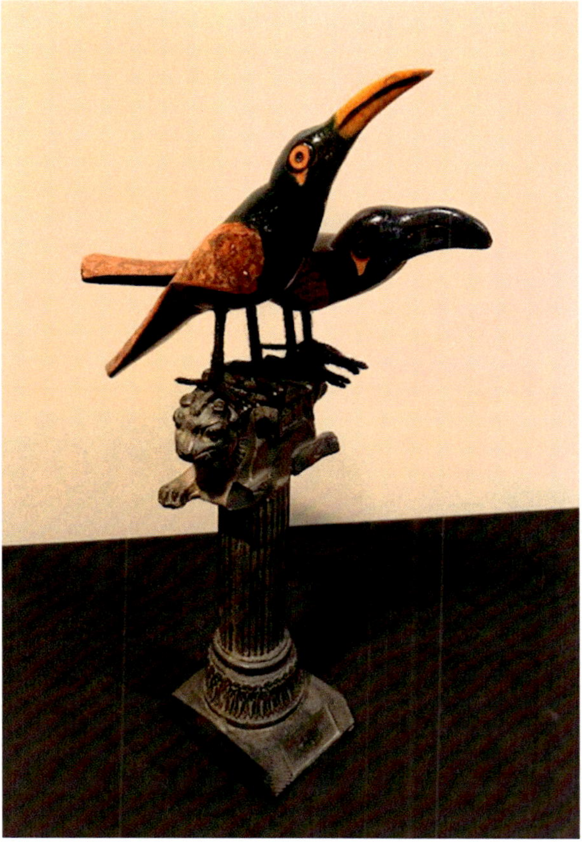

topping waves

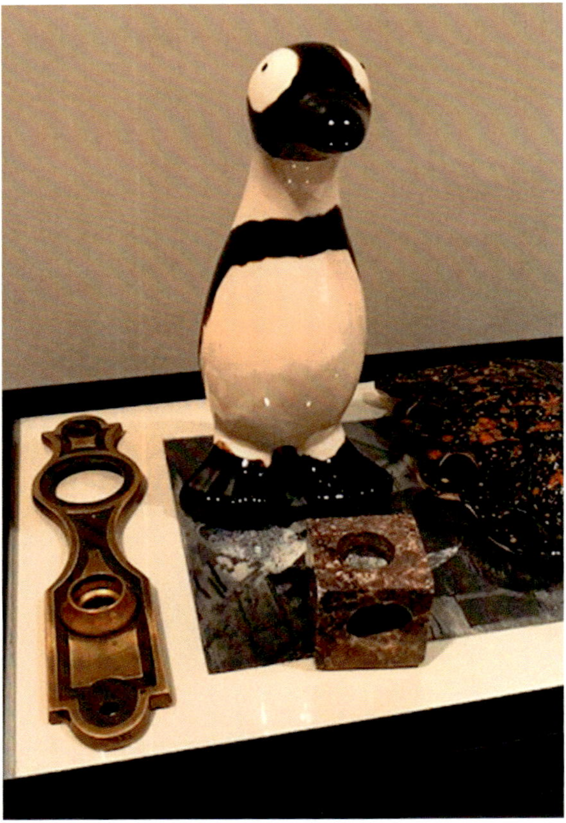

holed with dangers

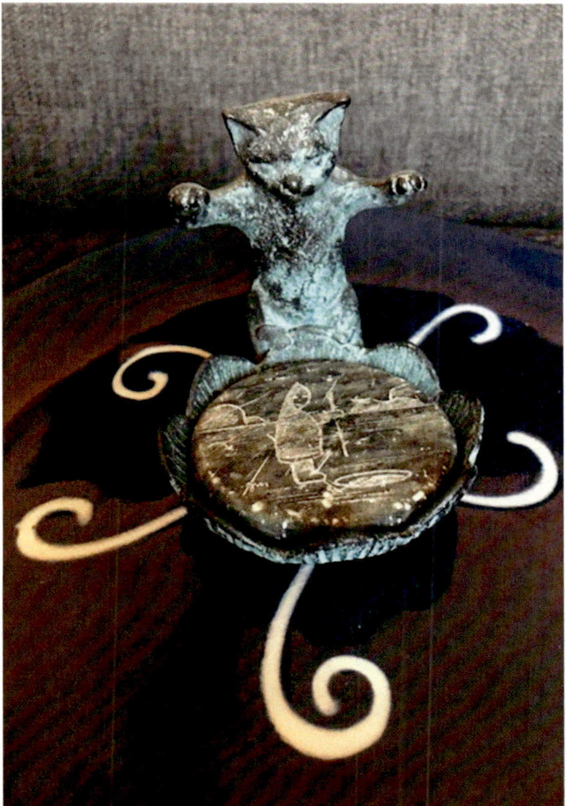

as imagined,

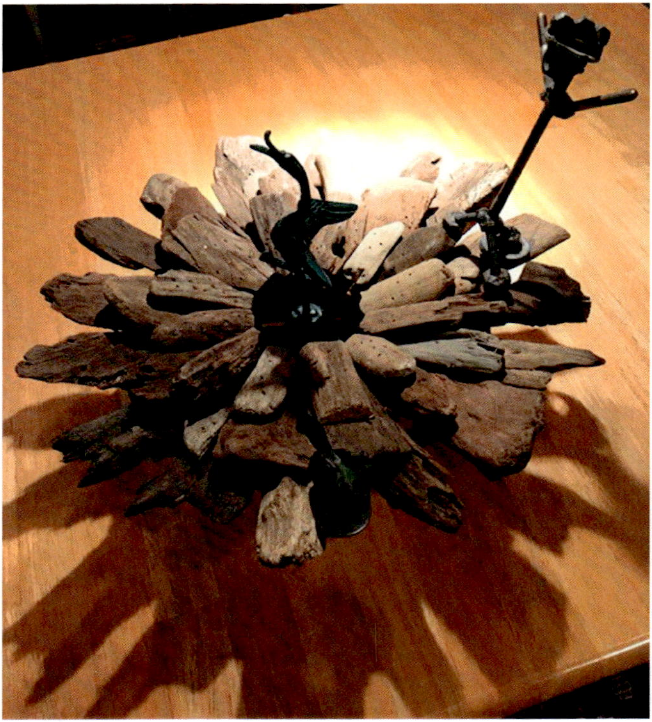

as imagined larger.

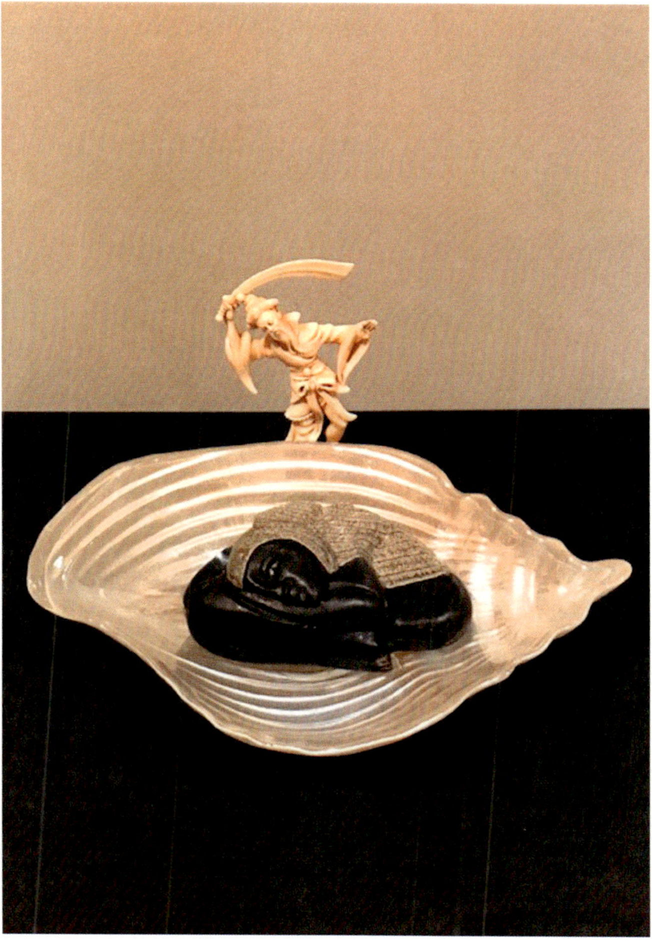

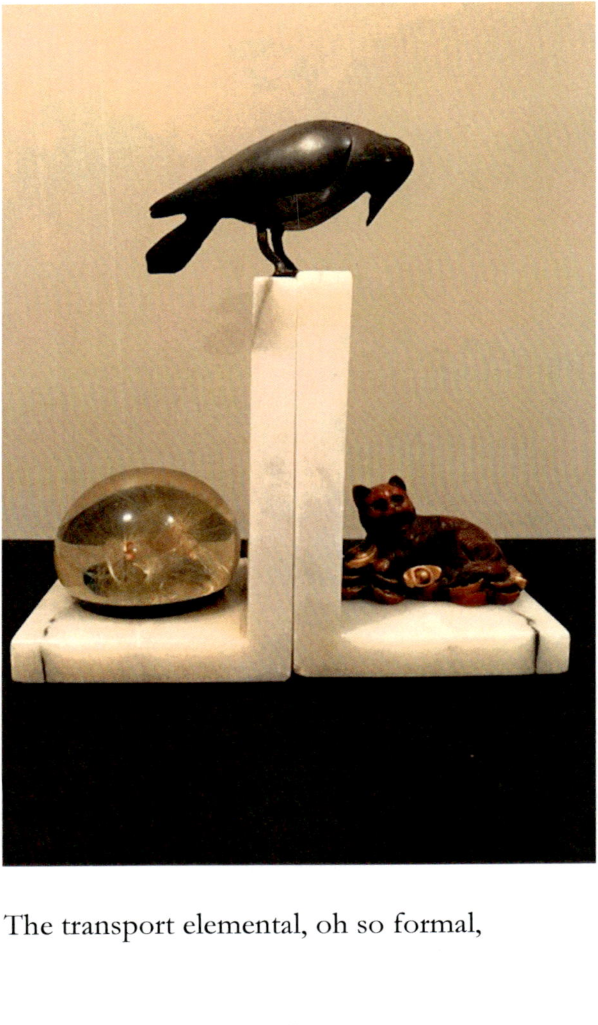

The transport elemental, oh so formal,

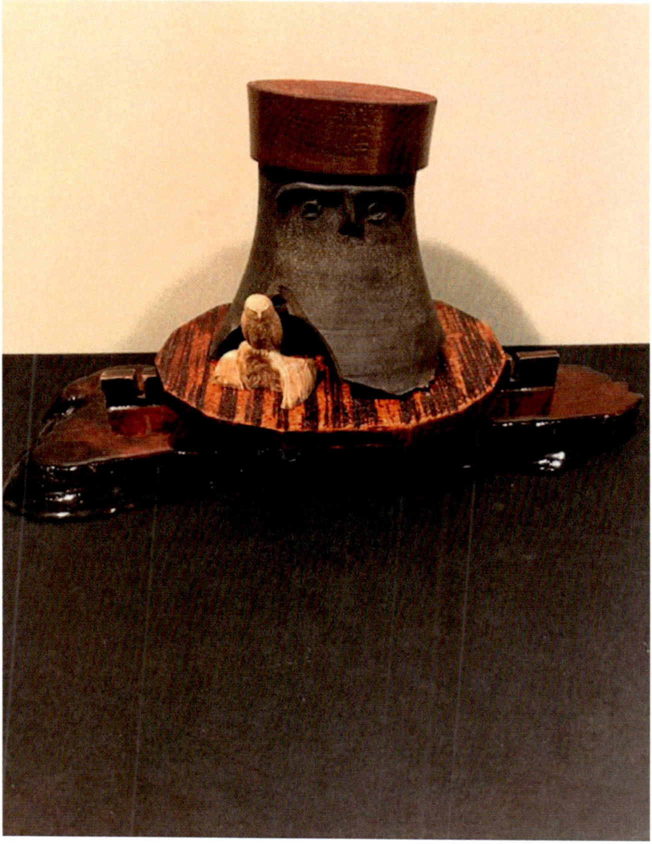

suggestive,

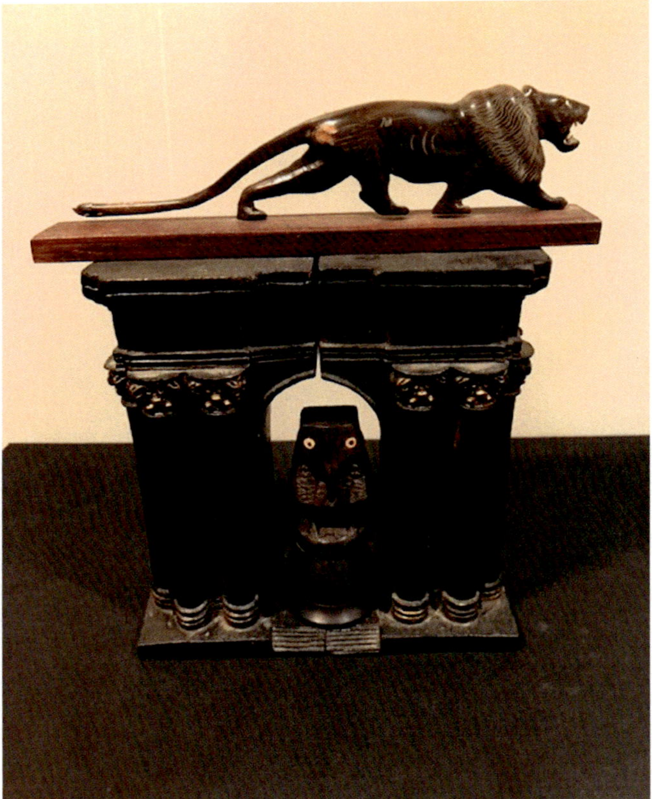

transitive, intransitive.

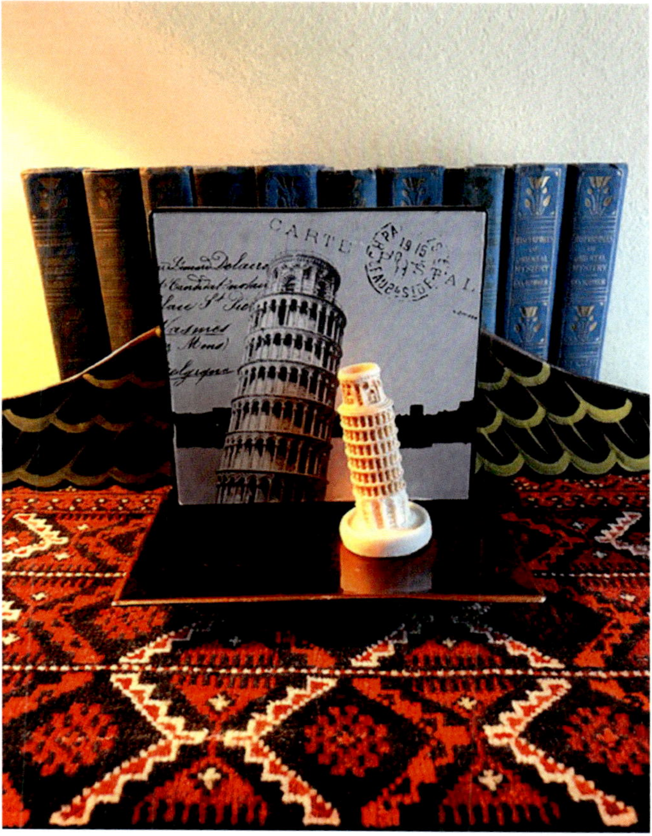

Mortal its wet wounds.

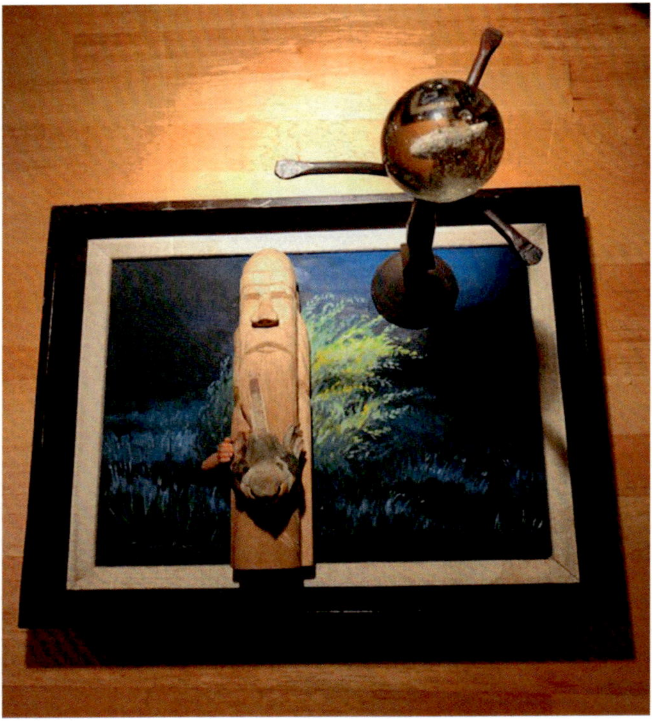

The letting go, slow—

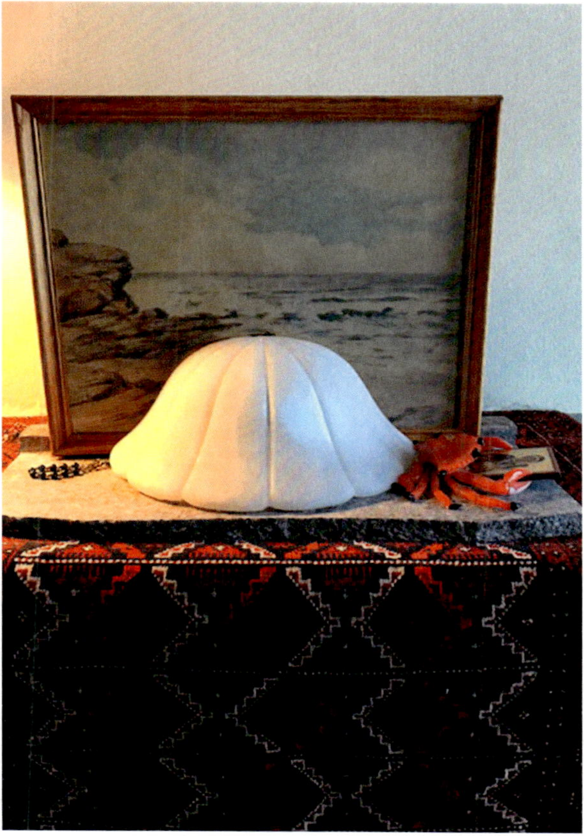

most transformative of forces.

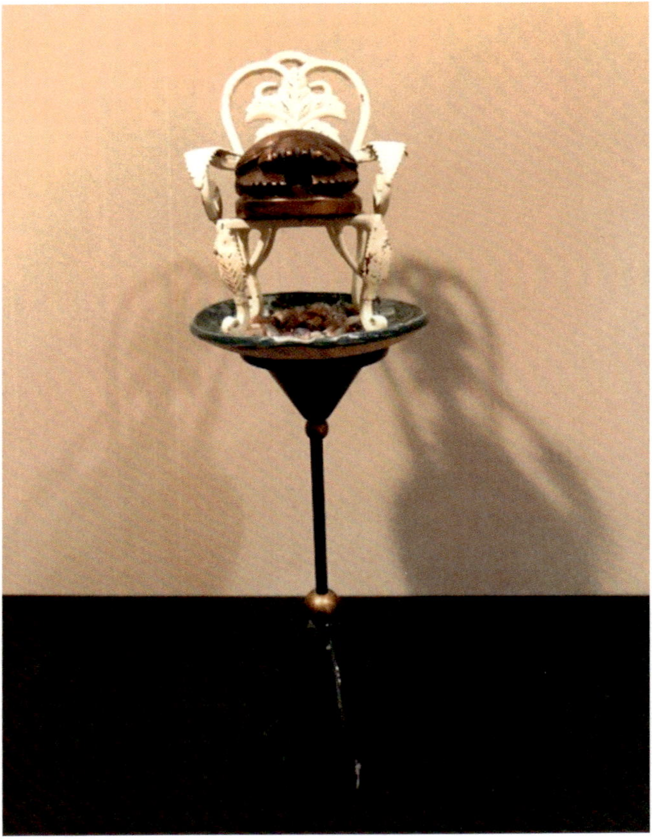

And after a meal of Infinity it sits.

The Natatorium

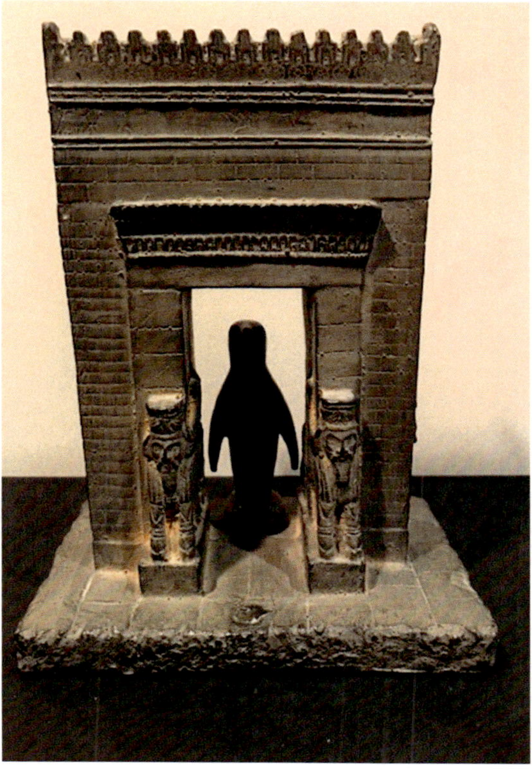

It would be carrying winter in your hand

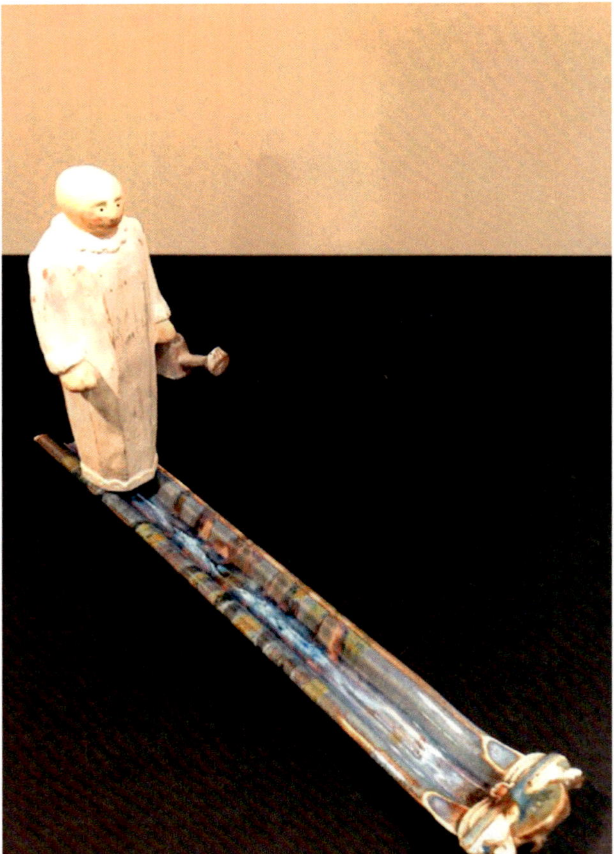

always;

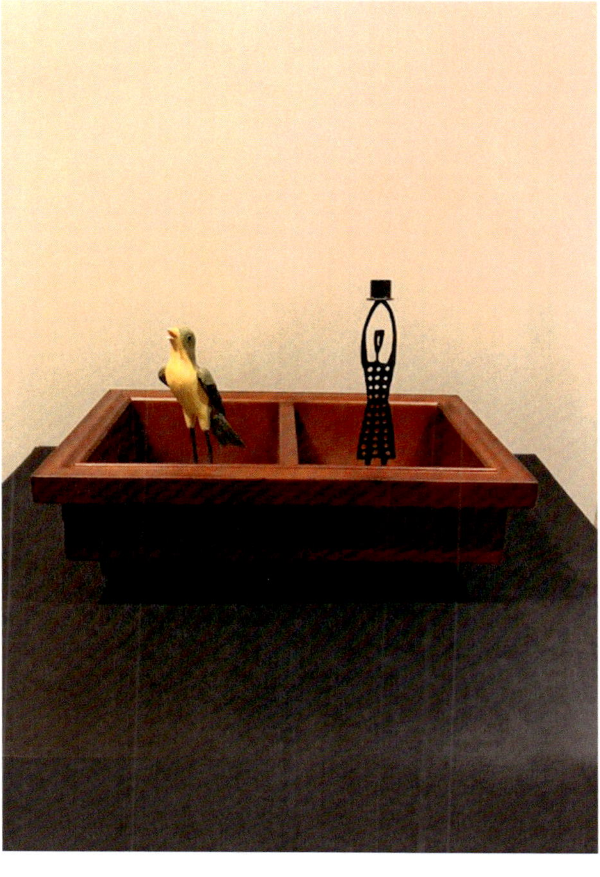

not the hand that waves,

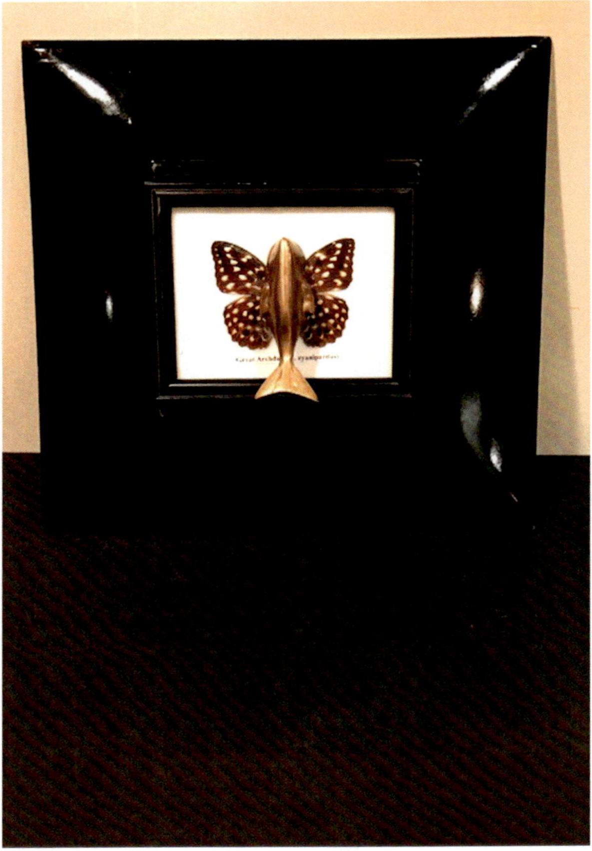

not the happy one,

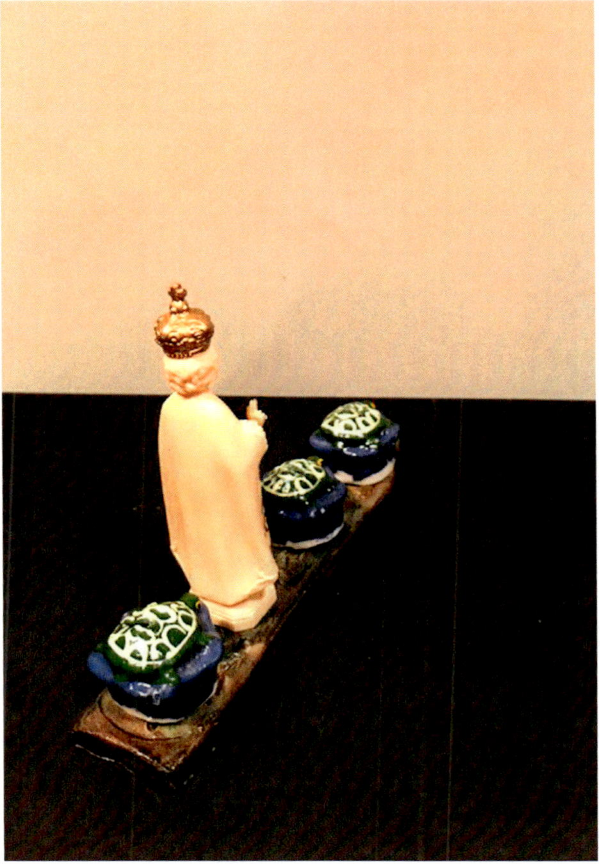

not the one busily restoring the crashed desktop

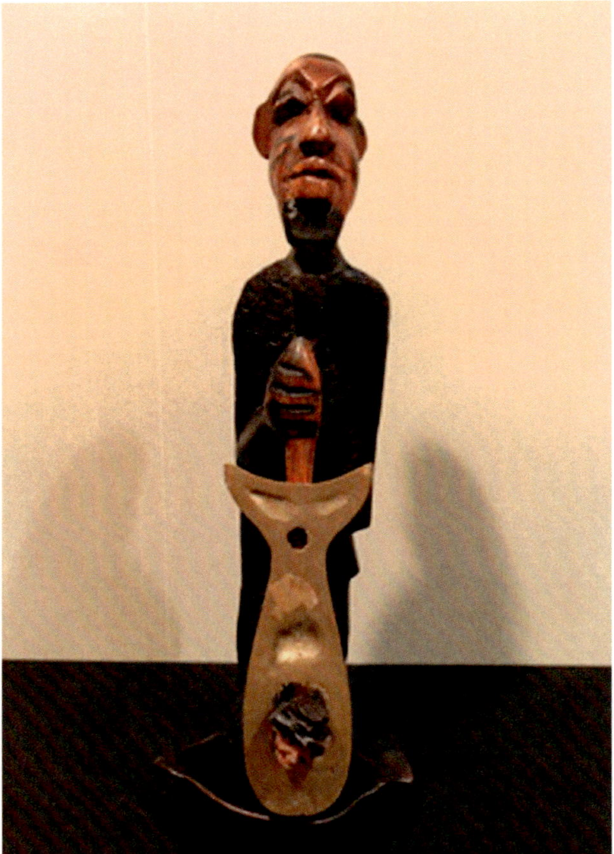

after it stops spinning—

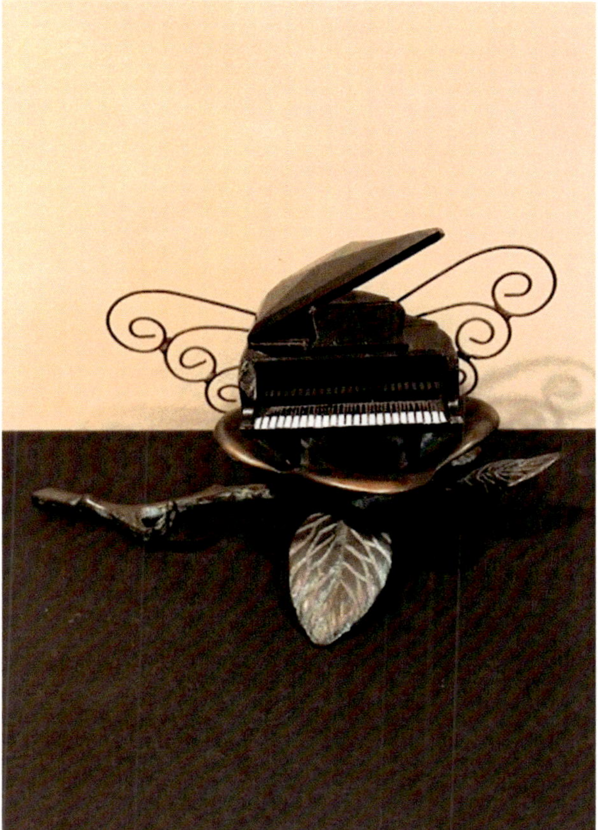

restacking its beehive boxes;

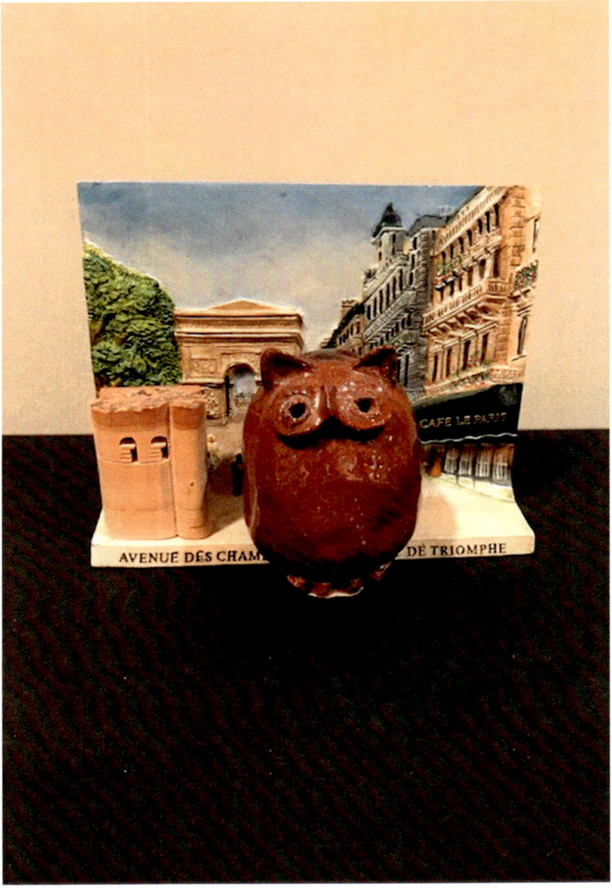

not that, but the one that waits

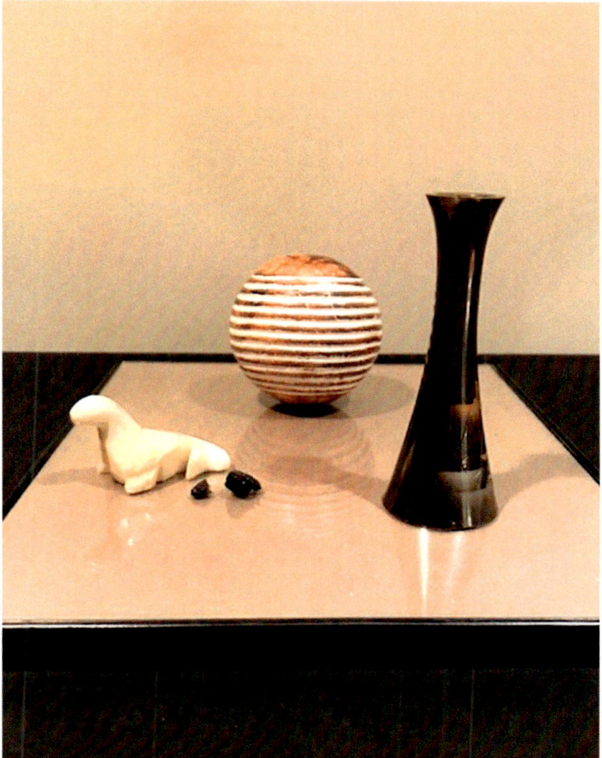

and waits—

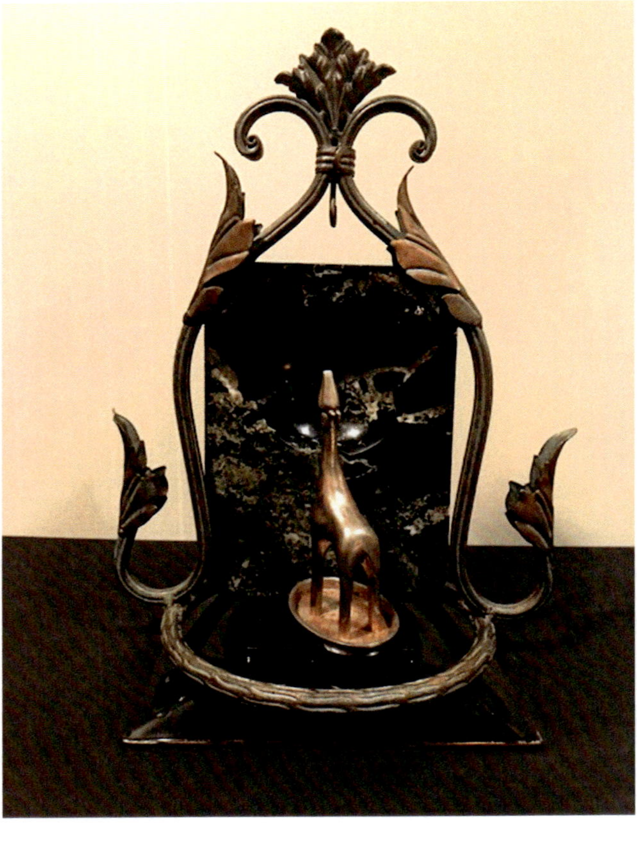

for the unresponsive

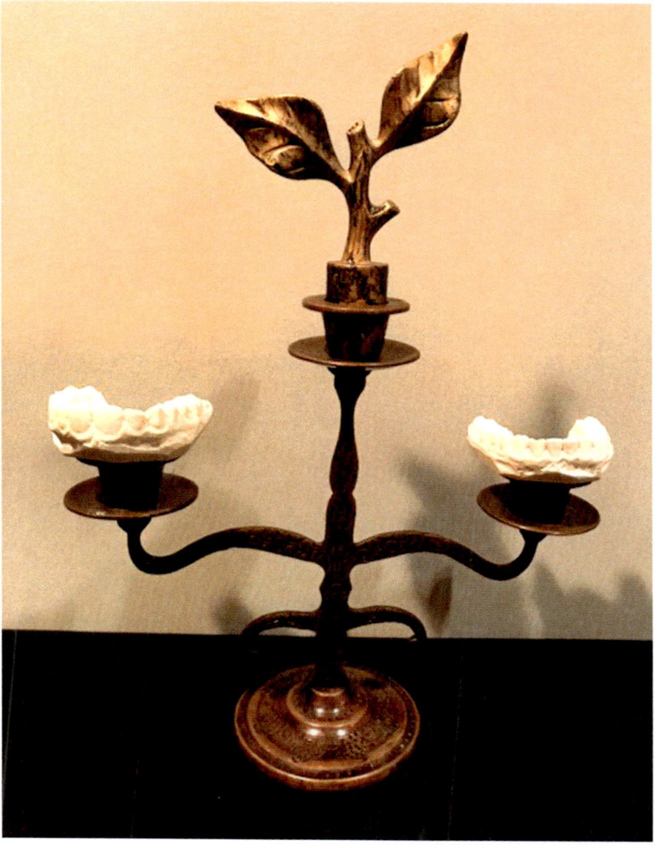

in the passivity pool—

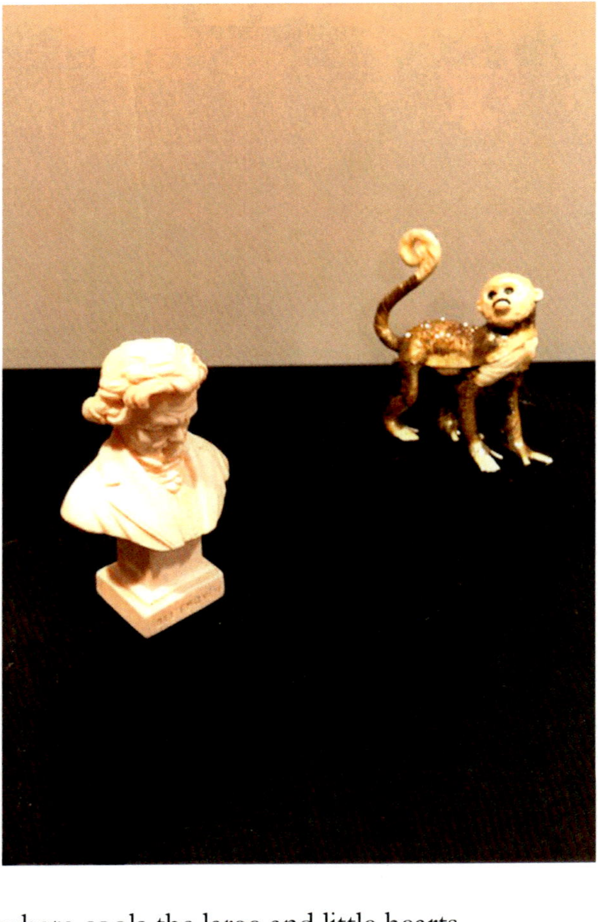

where cools the large and little hearts,

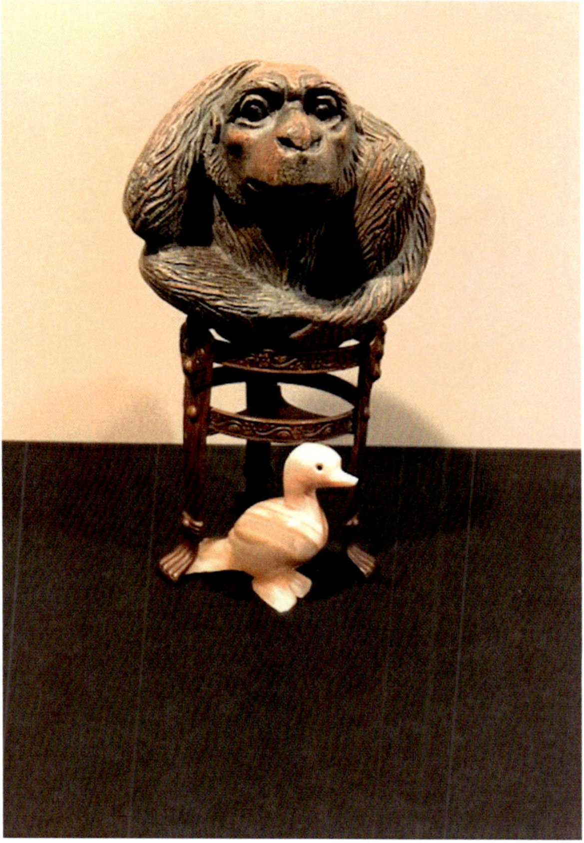

out of range,

and roaming.

Biographies & Acknowledgments

Neila Mezynski has exhibited since the early '90s on the West Coast and the East, in solo and group shows, most recently in the Bay area. Recent galleries include Gallery Sam (Oakland), 3rd St. Village Gallery (San Francisco), Smith and Jones Gallery (New York.) She was Artist in Residence at the Frederick Spratt Gallery, San Jose, in 2005.

Cooper Renner is the author of *Mosefolket*, *Disbelief* and *Florid Victorian Ornament*, all from Ravenna; co-author/illustrator of *Triple No. 1*; and author/illustrator of *The Tommy Plans* from Spuyten Duyvil.

Kathryn Rantala is the author of *3 Letters & Julius, The Finnish Orchestra, The Plant Waterer*, and others. The previously uncollected images here follow her assemblage series, *The Orphans of Thor Street; Small Bones, Little Fish; No Arc But the Luminous.* She is the editor of Ravenna Press and lives in Edmonds, Washington.